# A Mutual Friend

Peter Robinson was born in Salford, Lancashire, in 1953 and grew up mainly in Liverpool. He has degrees from the universities of York and Cambridge. After teaching for many years in Japan, he returned to Europe in 2007 and is currently Professor of English and American Literature at the University of Reading. The poetry editor for Two Rivers Press, author of many books of poetry, translations, prose, and literary criticism, he is married with two daughters.

# A Mutual Friend

## Poems for Charles Dickens

edited by Peter Robinson
with an Introduction by Adrian Poole

with the English Association

First published in the UK in 2012
by Two Rivers Press with the English Association
7 DENMARK ROAD, READING, RG1 5PA
www.tworiverspress.com

Copyright © Two Rivers Press 2012
Editorial matter and selection copyright © Peter Robinson 2012
Introduction copyright © Adrian Poole 2012
Individual poems copyright © the authors 2012

ISBN 978-1-901677-78-2

1 2 3 4 5 6 7 8 9

British Library Cataloguing in Publication Data. A catalogue record
for this book is available from the British Library.

Two Rivers Press is represented in the UK by Inpress Ltd
and distributed by Central Books Ltd.

Cover illustration and lettering © Martin Andrews 2012
Text design by Nadja Guggi and typeset in Pollen

Printed and bound in Great Britain by Imprint Digital, Exeter.

# Preface

I'm haunted by young Blight, the clerk in Mortimer Lightwood's office who relieves the boredom and shame of his employer's client-lack by ringing alphabetical changes on names: 'Mr. Halley, Mr. Lalley. Mr. Malley. And Mr. Boffin.' This could be the writer of *Our Mutual Friend* experimenting with initial consonants in search of characters' names – or equally, a poet finding rhymes. That Dickens himself refers to Blight's own christening as 'appropriate', finessing its obviousness by bigging it up, and that he characterizes so memorably Blight's verbal inventions as 'this fiction of an occupation', suggests the presence of authorial identification with the 'dismal boy' and his seemingly dismal fate. Dickens had worked as a clerk in a lawyers' office in Holborn from 1827 to 1828, learning shorthand in his spare time as a preparation for the journalism that would lead him to his vocation.

Reading Mr Boffin's interview with Blight for the first time during my first job, as a temporary lecturer, I found Dickens's picture of his clerk returning an echo. The Golden Dustman encourages Blight to keep pressing on – as Dickens himself had done by turning that 'fiction of an occupation' into his occupation of fiction. The novels are full of such encounters, occurring at a tangent to the works' main drift. Coming from oblique angles helps explain why they remain lodged in our memories. For Fernando Pessoa's heteronym, Bernardo Soares, also a clerk, in *The Book of Disquiet*: 'One of my life's greatest tragedies is to have already read *The Pickwick Papers*. (I can't go back and read them for the first time.)' For me, it's *Our Mutual Friend* ... which partly explains why I adapted its title for this tribute to its author, Charles Dickens, on his two-hundredth anniversary.

I can't recall how the notion of this anthology came to me, but it was after visiting West Wycombe Park in July 2008 where, as chance would have it, the BBC were filming a new serial adaptation of *Little Dorrit* – and all credit to those who arranged for this novel to be done at that moment, for above all else it is a circling around debt and the bankrupt banker, Merdle. Once again came the feeling that Dickens had already written the life we were playing, with that English country house as a beautiful backdrop for the differently unfolding circumstances of our new *Hard Times*. There was gratitude and indebtedness, and the need, only too present these days, to pay back our way. The debts are not only to Dickens and his illustrators, but to all the film-makers whose versions have provided an introduction to his characters and plots. And I see from the BFI's *Dickens Before Sound* collection that not only did he respond to 'magic lantern' story telling, but that adaptations of his works for the screen were first exhibited barely a decade after the novelist's death in 1870.

Nor is it inappropriate that *A Mutual Friend: Poems for Charles Dickens* should have Reading as its place of publication. The Thames valley was very much part of Dickens's extended territory. The George Inn still advertises itself as the place he would stay when visiting. The town almost persuaded him to stand as its MP. Around 1858 he established his mistress, the actress Ellen Ternan, just down the A4 from us in Slough. Dickens was present in Reading during 1843 when he gave a reading at the Literary, Scientific and Mechanics' Institute in London Street. Now the Great Expectations Hotel & Bar, its neo-classical Bath stone façade provides the cover for this anthology in a reproduction of Martin Andrews's painting.

So, speaking of debts, I would like to thank Pamela Bickley and Helen Lucas of the English Association for agreeing to support and collaborate in the making of this bicentennial homage. I'm grateful to the editorial team of Two Rivers Press for their collaborative attention to detail throughout the book's production. But first and foremost, my thanks go to the more than fifty poets whose work is published here. They have responded to the challenge of writing on Dickensian themes with enthusiasm, and have produced an extraordinarily varied set of contributions – while those in receipt of my editorial qualms were without exception graciously attentive. Finally, I would like to thank Adrian Poole for the kindness of his introduction.

*PETER ROBINSON*

# Contents

# Introduction

> Dickens's figures belong to poetry, like figures of Dante or Shakespeare, in that a single phrase, either by them or about them, may be enough to set them wholly before us ... Dickens can with a phrase make a character as real as flesh and blood – *'What a life young Bailey's was!'*[1]

High praise from T.S. Eliot in 1927, returning with interest Dickens's commendation of the poet's grandfather, Reverend William Greenleaf Eliot, on his visit to America, as 'a gentleman of great worth and excellence'. This makes him sound less fun than the young bootboy at Todgers's in *Martin Chuzzlewit*, 'with a large red head and no nose to speak of', and endless powers of survival. On such nobodies, Eliot claims, his author could shower a mythic grace as enduring as that conferred by Dante on Farinata and Shakespeare on Cleopatra. Eliot remembers Enobarbus remembering the Egyptian Queen: 'I saw her once / Hop forty paces through the public street'. One of young Bailey's talents is to execute 'a dancing step, extremely difficult in its nature, and only to be achieved in a moment of ecstasy, which is commonly called The Frog's Hornpipe' (*Martin Chuzzlewit,* ch.11). Searching for an appropriate way to deflate the 'pure bombast' of Julia Ward Howe's recitation of the 'Battle Hymn of the Republic', the young Eliot compared it to Mrs Leo Hunter's 'Ode to an Expiring Frog' in *Pickwick Papers* (ch.15). More solemnly, in 1917 he imagined an equivalence in the consuming effect of the ongoing war to Richard Carstone's obsession with Chancery in *Bleak House*. A year later he told his mother he was looking forward to lecturing on Dickens.[2] Not so surprising after all then that *The Waste Land* should boast one of the great might-have-been titles, lifted from Dickens's last completed novel, 'He do the police in different voices'.

1  T.S. Eliot, *Selected Essays* (London: Faber and Faber, 1951), p.462.
2  References in this paragraph are to *The Letters of T.S. Eliot*, ed. Valerie Eliot and Hugh Haughton, vol.I: 1898–1922, Revised Edition (London: Faber and Faber, 2009), pp.4n, 99, 188, 249.

There is an aptness to this volume's chosen title, *A Mutual Friend*, to which many of its contributors have responded. Its sub-title might well be 'They do Dickens in different voices'. *Our Mutual Friend* is a novel that speaks to them as it did to Eliot, perhaps above all for the mighty river that runs through the city, brimming with the drowned bodies that pollute Spenser's 'Sweet Thames'. Not only the river but also the dust-heaps, the rubbish and waste, excess and excrescence, and the usual swelling cast of characters with outrageously indelible or stealthily adhesive names, falling into patterns even as one writes them:

Wegg, Wilfer, Venus, Veneering,
Wren, Wrayburn, Riderhood, Headstone ...

Dickens read and listened to verse with more enthusiasm for the humorous and the sentimental than for the elevated and complex ambitions of his friend Tennyson's *In Memoriam* or Browning's *Men and Women*. His taste was closer to Dick Swiveller's in *The Old Curiosity Shop* than to Eugene Wrayburn's in *Our Mutual Friend*. Shakespeare of course was a different matter, a poet to be sure in the largest sense of the word, but also a popular dramatist, and more immediately for Dickens and other nineteenth-century writers a story-teller and creator of characters, not simply larger than life, like Falstaff, Cleopatra, and Lear, but summoned to life by a single phrase: 'What is honour? A word', 'No more but e'en a woman', 'Pray you, undo this button'.

Dickens did write verse, both published and unpublished, including three songs for *Pickwick Papers*, some political squibs for *The Examiner* and *The Daily News*, prologues for plays by Westland Marston and Wilkie Collins.[3] Here's a taste of the satirical verse, from 'The Fine Old English Gentleman', in 1841:

3 See the helpful entries on 'Poetry and poets before Dickens', 'Poetry and poets during Dickens's life-time', and 'Poetry by Dickens', in the *Oxford Reader's Companion to Dickens*, ed. Paul Schlicke (Oxford: Oxford University Press, 1999), pp.455–6.

The good old times for cutting throats that cried out in their need,
The good old times for hunting men who held their fathers' creed,
The good old times when William Pitt, as all good men agreed,
Came down direct from Paradise at more than railway speed ...
Oh, the fine old English Tory times;
When will they come again!

And another, of the melodrama on which he enthusiastically collaborated with Collins, from 'The Song of the Wreck' (*The Lighthouse*, 1855):

The wind blew high, the waters raved,
  A ship drove on the land,
A hundred human creatures saved
  Kneel'd down upon the sand.
Three-score were drown'd, three-score were thrown
  Upon the black rocks wild,
And thus among them, left alone,
  They found one helpless child.[4]

It is not on writing like this that his claims to immortality rest. If we need reminding what they *do* depend on, we could listen to the poetry of a passage such as this, from *Bleak House* (ch. 40), with its wonderfully intricate rhythms and cadences:

This present summer evening, as the sun goes down, the preparations are complete. Dreary and solemn the old house looks, with so many appliances of habitation, and with no inhabitants except the pictured forms upon the walls. So did these come and go, a Dedlock in possession might have ruminated passing along; so did they see this gallery hushed and quiet, as I see it now; so think, as I think, of the gap that they would make in this domain when they were gone; so find it, as I find it, difficult to believe that it could

4 *Complete Plays and Selected Poems of Charles Dickens* (London: Vision Press, 1970), pp. 229, 241.

be, without them; so pass from my world, as I pass from theirs, now closing the reverberating door; so leave no blank to miss them, and so die.

The later novels have provoked more new utterance in this volume than earlier fictions such as *Pickwick Papers* (1837), *Nicholas Nickleby* (1839) or indeed *Martin Chuzzlewit* (1844). W. H. Auden thought the real theme of *Pickwick Papers* was 'the Fall of Man'. What makes Pickwick a mythical character is that he does not fall from innocence into sin: 'he changes from an innocent child into an innocent adult who no longer lives in an imaginary Eden but in the real and fallen world'.[5] Modern readers and writers have less faith in such improbably enduring innocence. It is the real and fallen world, especially of the later, darker works towards which they are most urgently drawn, from *Dombey and Son* (1848) to the unfinished *Mystery of Edwin Drood* (1870). Works that are, to our eyes and ears, prophetic of the dark powers of a monster metropolis and the world that orbits around it, the dreams and nightmares it inspires, the promises it makes and breaks, the real horrors and consolations it produces: *Bleak House* (1853) in particular (which Eliot judged to be Dickens's 'best novel', or at least his 'finest piece of construction'), *Little Dorrit* (1857) and *Great Expectations* (1861). The poems gathered here bear vivid testimony to the life and death harboured by Dickens's London, under the pressure of which such harmless words as 'street', 'stairs' and 'stone', 'alleys and by-ways', seem to acquire new ominous meaning. Think of the phrase 'walk all night', and with Dickens in mind, it prompts a whole mental, emotional, psychic landscape. So too with the city's familiar structures and products as they decay into ruin and rubbish.

Another everyday word that takes on a special aura when it strays into Dickens's sphere of influence is 'child'. There are as many references to childhood and children in this volume as you'd expect, especially to the prospect of treats in store, to disappointments, to dreams and nightmares. 'Dickens' is a word associated with an older

---

5   W. H. Auden, 'Dingley Dell and the Fleet', *The Dyer's Hand and other essays* (London: Faber and Faber, 1963), pp. 408–9.

generation, with parents and teachers pressing on resistant youth 'a complete set' or a 'leather-bound edition', teasing the ear with old-fashioned phrases such as 'what the dickens' and 'mutton chops'. This menace is mild compared to what lies truly in wait for the vulnerable reader, the murder of Nancy for instance, and Quilp and Carker and Murdstone and so on. Under Dickens's spell all readers are vulnerable, reduced to enduring as well as enjoying 'the eye of childhood' (to borrow from Lady Macbeth). Local council web-sites engage now in properly earnest definition of the 'vulnerable adult'; reference to the complete works of Charles Dickens would not come amiss.

'A single phrase, either by them or about them'. Yet prior to this are the very names. To read the poems in this volume is to be struck afresh by the mesmeric force in Dickens's names, or perhaps even more in the act of naming, so imperative is the itch to utter them aloud, over and over. What a menagerie of gruesome creatures is invoked by the very sound of the words: Twist, Heep, Squeers, Cratchit, Scrooge, Gamp, Gradgrind, Grewgious, Dedlock, Merdle, Drummle, Havisham, Jaggers, Magwitch, Orlick, Fledgeby, Wegg, and so on and so on. What a relief in the mildness of a mere Pip and Pocket, a Tapley and Traddles, Trotwood, Micawber. What sadness in a Little Nell, her fate predicted in its homophone 'knell'; what modest resilience in a Little Dorrit.

In fact the evidence of the poems here suggests that Eliot may not have been quite right in suggesting that it is the single phrase 'by or about' a character that sets them wholly before us. We need to draw out the potential in the deceptively simple preposition 'about'. Young Bailey after all, for all his mythic significance, is a relatively minor figure in his novel, as Barkis, with his legendary willingness, is in *David Copperfield*. What seems to matter to the poets in this volume is not so much the phrases closely attached to particular characters. These poems are packed with Dickens's own words, phrases, often whole sentences, and on one occasion at least an extended passage ingeniously rendered into verse. These words do not belong to specific characters so much as the characters belong to them, for this is a whole world of words in which they struggle to live, from which to escape, amongst which to find refuge, contentment, the occasional garden. Quite ordinary words, as I've suggested, but also of course more resonant ones, such as 'ivy green', 'kite', 'donkeys', 'fog', 'evening mists', 'forge', 'lime-kiln', 'Ghost's Walk', 'the Grand Canal', 'even supposing—'. Or phrases that begin to sound like Dickens's whether they actually are so or not, like 'scavenging people' or 'found in the river'.

Most striking however is the extraordinary range of words and phrases that have provoked these poets, from which they launch off, around which they spin. Many of the following will be promptly recognized by intimate readers of Dickens, but it will take a special or specialist ear to place exactly where they all come from – a party game, such as Dickens himself might well have enjoyed. Here goes: 'mumchance', 'a long row of new square brick boxes', 'the flitting shapes and shadows of my dismal entering reverie', 'like a mournful echo of things that lie in my own heart', 'I wear the chain I forged in life', 'Oh, my lungs and liver, what do you want? Oh, goroo, goroo!', 'as if they were up in a balloon', 'intelligence is weak in English', 'some consolation in walls', 'his ventures had been utterly reckless', 'a wrapped up man coming through the gate', 'scented soap', 'God bless you, God forgive you!', 'this fiction of an occupation', 'Another mortal struggle, and he was up again, beating the water with his hands', 'Is she like you? She must be very beautiful', 'between Southwark Bridge which is of iron, and London Bridge which is of stone'.

These and many other words of Dickens live again in the poems that follow, attracting weird, wonderful and magical transformations, such as would have delighted their originator. And indeed the poet who liked to lift things and out of them make something new: 'Sweet Thames run softly ...'.

ADRIAN POOLE

# A Mutual Friend

Poems for Charles Dickens

# Do you like Dickens?

You had a rival, that long-ago summer in Youghal,
The bookshop owner's creepy son with his funeral suit
And his dandruff, wringing his hands with lust
While the girl swam chastely up and down the pool.

All week you brooded on the manner of his death,
Until matters were taken out of your hands by her mother.
'So, Maurice, do you like Dickens?' 'Oh yes.' Creep creep.
'For example?' A pause.' ... *A Christmas Carol*?' 'And?'

And off he crept. You knew there was a reason why
You took *Great Expectations* everywhere,
The night Estella came to find you in the outhouse.

You were a poor boy, a paperback, suitable
Only for poolside amusement. What did she call it?
The common pursuit: but she read you from cover to cover.

*SEAN O'BRIEN*

# Dickens and My Father

Thackeray he liked but Dickens he loved.
Clothes came out of his rucksack to put in
*The Old Curiosity Shop, Barnaby Rudge*
Micawber, Oliver, Nell, Pip and Boz.

I wrote school essays, was praised. My father said
'Dickens is the very pinnacle of a novelist'
and then, lowering his voice, he affirmed
the life of a novelist entails sacrifice.

I imagined Dickens writing at his drawing room table
while little girls in voluminous skirts with sashes
romped with dogs and brothers. He wrote on
throwing words into the conversation the way

a fire blazes up from fresh logs.
Then I saw Doughty Street, clean and bare
pained somehow – it was mid-winter –
the grate, black-leaded, like a household god

the fire had gone from. Imagined Dickens
voyaging to America, fêted, bored
tired beyond measure. Still from each spoken
sentence sprang everything my father promised.

Everything there is: cities, streets, air, fug
Old Father Thames wearing Miss Havisham's fog
(at school we were writing about Transport.
What Dickens could have done with that!)

Choose anything and he's in it. Trees, boots,
mutton chops, hopes dashed, new beginnings
as many hearts as in hell or heaven
until this world of ours stops spinning.

*ELIZABETH SMITHER*

# The Dickens

*What the Dickens ...?* The Devil,
that is. I knew it from Aunt Edie's parlour: unbroached
    and forbidding shelves of him,

the complete set (every home
of substance had one) – him in oxblood leather
    with a dusty, taxidermy smell,

with gold-leaf titles branded in,
slick bricks of gilt-edged pages, cigarette-paper-thin
    yet heavier than paper should be,

him like a phalanx of family bibles ...
but what spilled out, at my stray first opening, when
    the grown-ups' backs were turned,

was a much of muchness, Boz
and Phiz and fizzog, tic and pose and cringe and leer
    cramped into shadowy vignettes

like nether places – faces, yes,
of torment, there where we've no choice but be
    ourselves condensed beyond hope,

our very names contorted to a rictus,
Twist, Heep, Squeers, Cratchit – an eternity of nicknames
    jeered by who but ... Old Nick? (Was

that Nicholas? Or Nickleby?) Or what
the Dickens am I doing – six years old, there, scared
    to look away or turn the page, and

        here, still, fifty years on, writing this?

*PHILIP GROSS*

# Three Sonnets for Dickens

i.m. Angus Wilson

1 *Boz in Newgate*
November 1835

Two lifeless shadows haunt the lower cell,
Denied what sympathy we grant the living.
Already in an anteroom of Hell,
They feel the glare of God the Unforgiving.

Convicted of a crime the news reports
Deodorise in Latin or leave nameless,
Unworthy of the mercy of the courts –
Suppose such cryptic brotherhood were blameless ...

How can it be, the cockroach and the rat
Seem innocent, while men consensus shames
Attract a sentence with no caveat?

The sullen gaoler never says their names;
But, once the trap has dropped, will Smith and Pratt
Allow us the impertinence of John and James?

2 *Pip on Herbert Pocket*

I was a mirror to abuse,
            Engaged by fate or accident.
He being privileged to choose
            A fight without an argument,
It seemed unfriendly to refuse.
            More vigorous than violent,
He'd no aggression to excuse.
            His shyness was so confident!

For even bruises do unbruise
        And quitting would be negligent.
He needed me. With Mars as muse,
        Inspired to take his punishment,
With me to lose to, glad to lose –
        He seemed so brave and innocent!

*3 Smike's Surmise*

'A sister!' Friendship's not a fire
but something safer, dimmer, cooler.
Provoking neither swank nor fear,
its lesser Eros is as callow
as buds the ice starts melting for.
You watch a man above the collar
and his impassive nape, though fair,
acquires a fleeting dash of colour.

The one of two unequals who
desires is less inclined to pull
his punches. Quick to see what's true,
his logic unimpeachable,
he asks his friend, 'Is she like you?
She must be very beautiful.'

    *GREGORY WOODS*

5

# Ivy

after Charles Dickens's 'The Ivy Green'

Like a long silk scarf mysteriously drawn
from the magician's empty top hat,

she climbs upwards from the dark earth;
an evergreen and ever-growing vine.

Old panes of glass give way to her touch
no louder than the *click* of a key in a lock.

Half-snake, half-bird she creeps, she steals
across the floors and then takes flight –

winding the worm-eaten leg of a chair,
rewriting the floral designs on the walls.

For her, each abandoned home in this town
is a gingerbread house she'll slowly consume

with her aerial roots: a thousand tongues
savouring mortar, morsels of stone.

*ISABEL GALLEYMORE*

# At a Public Reading by Charles Dickens

Tell us about Copperfield and Oliver
And his wishing for the dishing out of more
Let's hear about the optimist Micawber
And his persistent hopes of what lay up afore
Do divulge of Mister Scrooge and poor Miss Havisham
That disenchanted woman who set her world alight
Tell us any of your stories that you fancy
But please don't tell us Nancy's tale tonight

Let your prose expose social conditions
Where there should be improvement of the plight
Tell us and impel us to correction
To protection and to setting things aright
Perhaps pick one of Mister Pickwick's papers
Dingley Dell at Christmastime for instance
But please don't tell us Nancy's tale tonight

Don't spill the beans of her and Bill
Don't put your public through the mill
Mr Dickens as you will
Yes, as you fancy, up until
That villainy and villain all contrite
Let common sympathy prevail
Leave us hearty, leave us hale
And please don't tell us Nancy's tale tonight

*JOHN HEGLEY*

# Damage

Let me break up the lines.
    There's moonlight now.
Wet London cobbles.  Shadows,
     the stink of frying onions.
Red haired, in raggy night gear,
     a merry old gentleman
offers friendship, sausages, hot gin
     to his pack of street children:
his family workshop warmer
     than the workhouse.

'My dear,' he croons, 'my dear,'
     and soon that voice is in our ears,
genius gives him life, he is loose
     in our imagination,
an 'out and outer' tapping into centuries
     of thieving peddlers.
Cruikshank gives him a woolly caftan
     cross-hatched for texture,
stands him by the fire
     with a toasting fork, like the devil.
Bill Sikes' brutality is local English.

As Fagin cowers in his cell, waiting to be
     hanged, there are some puzzles:
his name, for instance – Irish, not Ashkenazi –
     and a Bob Fagin kind to young Charles
in the blacking factory.  The choice
     is part of a writer's dream,

which has its own rules of vitality,
     like the gestures of caricature;
no wakeful effort to correct the damage
     by drawing Riah can begin to cure.

*ELAINE FEINSTEIN*

# Old Wyldes

1

Old Wyldes is a former farmhouse on the southwest border of Hampstead Garden Suburb, close to the Old Bull and Bush and the phantom tube station (North End) whose unfinished platform is still visible between Hampstead and Golders Green on the Northern Line. I grew up round there and have often walked with friends to see the house before or after tea at Golders Hill Park across the road.

William Blake regularly visited his friend John Linnell at Old Wyldes, staying over on at least one occasion, according to the blue plaque on the house, which is still a private residence. In 1837, ten years after Blake's death, Dickens and his wife rented the house for a few weeks, while recovering from the death of Mary Hogarth, the novelist's sister-in-law and a key woman in his life. Dickens was working on *Oliver Twist* during this period, and it was published the following year. Bill Sikes will show up in this part of Hampstead, on the run after murdering Nancy. Surely Dickens walked around here during that fortnight and recycled a specific memory, not the less imagined for that: *Traversing the hollow by the Vale of Health, he mounted the opposite bank, and crossing the road which joins the villages of Hampstead and Highgate, made along the remaining portion of the heath to the fields at North End, in one of which he laid himself down under a hedge, and slept.*

2

My father's oldest friend Philip Lewis and his wife Lily gave me a complete set of Dickens for my barmitzvah in 1955. The books came from Boots (in those days a library and bookshop as well as a chemists) in Piccadilly Circus or Regent Street: I knew this because a volume was missing and I went to collect it. Some years later, I realised my presents had been orchestrated by my father, since people would not have known to give me books. However, I did receive three fountain pens: 'Today I am a fountain pen,' in the words of the old joke about the barmitzvah boy's party speech. Fagin and Riah: did they too have a barmitzvah? (How many children had Lady Macbeth?) The characters from *Oliver Twist* and *Our Mutual Friend* fit perfectly this extract from the interview that apparently took place between Dostoevsky and Dickens: *There were two people in him, he told me: one who feels as he ought to feel and one who feels the opposite. From the one who feels the opposite I make my evil characters, from the one who feels as a man ought to feel I try to live my life. Only two people? I asked.*

3

Literary associations with Dickens are legion:

*Item*: Dickens and Balzac both influenced Dostoevsky.

*Item*: Evelyn Waugh's childhood house is about two hundred yards from Old Wyldes: 145 North End Road, Golders Green, NW11. He would walk up the hill to post his letters in NW3. Waugh's father was a partner in Chapman and Hall, which published Dickens and Evelyn himself.

*Item*: Kafka's *Metamorphosis* – Paula Rego painted me as the cockroach – parodies Dickens.

*Item*: Melville's *Bartleby*, according to Borges, foreshadows Kafka and recapitulates Dickens.

*Item*: Poe's famous bird, originally a parrot, was inspired by the raven in *Barnaby Rudge*. Reversed, the first two syllables of 'Nevermore' echo 'raven'.

*Item*: Rabbi Lionel Blue's dog was called Riah.

*Item*: Elizabeth Barrett Browning compared Balzac and Dickens as both reaching out hands to help suffering humanity, but in the case of Dickens they are *clean* hands.

4

As a student of French and Russian literature, I've read more novels by Balzac and Dostoevsky than by Dickens. That's not difficult, especially in the case of Balzac, who wrote nearly a hundred in thirty years. Dickens read, wrote and spoke French quite well. His first biographer Forster records him as saying he read Balzac. Bernard Berenson was sure that Eugène Sue and Victor Hugo influenced *Our Mutual Friend*. I'm now in my seventieth year: shall I find the time to read the Dickens novels I've not yet read? If so, what will become of my project to reread Dostoevsky? There is no time to lose.

*ANTHONY RUDOLF*

# My Mother's Lesson

In a bygone age
stuck for a house description
my mother cogged a page
from a leather-bound edition

of Dickens's tale of Nell
in another bygone age.
She did the job so well
the teacher turned the page

without noticing the craft
of Dickens's tale of Nell
or of my mother's graft.
Or was it Dingley Dell

she stitched into Mayo
with such unnoticed craft?
Write from what you know,
they say, draft after draft.

So someone else's mother
I've stitched into Mayo
with Nell and her big brother,
or Mr Winkle's crow.

Better a house description
with someone else's mother
so every last suspicion
can be cleverly smothered.

She taught me what I know:
better a house description
that hides the real tableau
and basks in sweet deception.

*JUSTIN QUINN*

# The Death of Little Nell

At nine Miss Casson came
to teach me sums and reading,
geography, history, scripture,
and also, as a treat,
to read the story of little Nell
while I drew pictures, unrelated
though somehow parallel:
flowers, a car, a pony, a woman in a hat.

The poor were always with you,
were not you, so I was taught.
They'd passed already on their way to school
and whooped and ran and climbed
our wall and swung on the drive gate
and pinched the berries from our rowan tree,
bullet-headed boys, barefoot,
or clutching a slab of bread and jam,
enviable free boys!

Nell was poor too. Her death was otherwise,
though nothing to do with me.
A story worked like that.
It was educational, like fractions.
No one asked me for the point,
that nothing was really different –
the times, the clothes, the fears,
hunger, disease, and lice: thus money.
There wasn't enough of that.

It didn't bother me, not yet.
I was just to bear in mind
behind Nell's death was pity, or its lack.

*MAIRI MACINNES*

# A Carol for Angus Reach

Narrow streets and courtyards, dark and damp behind
the commercial facades of London or Manchester
*I wear the chain I forged in life, I made it link by link*
odour of slopwater, distrust of strangers, fear of police
infant mortality 1830s urban 50% rural 33% *I see a vacant seat*
*and a crutch without an owner ...* 'men of cotton' who pass
'brooding, meditative lives', a great city under
the black shadow of Satan's wing, dragon breathing
of the steam engines, steel doors crashing shut,
crouched/aggressive walking postures *O God! to hear*
*the insect on the leaf pronouncing on the too much life*
*of his hungry brother!* and something whether fiction or
document starts a long quest, seeking a dim light from within,
like the dim glow of small coal fires deep in the town cellars,
a violent longing for the fresh air, space, and light of the mills
to spread through the houses, 'flinging open the cul-de-sacs'
*good deeds spring from the wound*

> What hope then? –

Cheap summer trips by railway, the Ten Hours Bill (1847)
'general good spirits of the operatives' possibly
something will come of this in the long term
*And he took a child, and set him in the midst of them.*

> 'Everybody is to blame.'
> *The kind heart trembled.*


*PETER RILEY*

# The Drowned Man

'Another mortal struggle, and he was up again,
 beating the water with his hands ...'
the death of Daniel Quilp from *The Old Curiosity Shop*

Up from the river bed, up from the slab,
Thames-rotten, slime-festooned, slow-
decomposed to uglier than any sideshow's
pennyworth, he's here, floating on his back:
a dead man leering at a tiled ceiling, eddying
after me. I'm pulling hard against clean water,
public, purified, it stings my lungs, *pull harder
or he'll reach me, drag me under with him, win.*

I know he cannot touch me, *felo-de-se*
a stake in his heart at a stopping place
where two roads cross. I know that earth
has done its work, that boot and wheel
have flattened, scree has ratified his death;
but still he surfaces, still lurks and follows,
winks, grimaces, breathes out the reek of devils.

*SUSAN UTTING*

# Quilp Rock

So when, just over a century later,
   in 1948,
the Falkland Islands Dependencies
   surveyors first beheld
an isolated hump in Labeuf Fjord –
   a mile and a half North West
   of the island of Pourquoi Pas –
it seemed the natural thing to those Dickensians

   to name it after Daniel.
Perhaps the pitiless seas in which it rose
   gave them a hint for its christening.
Perhaps the slavering tumulus suggested
   his last appearance,
careening off the fogbound wharf till the river
   'carried a corpse away.'

Or maybe it simply seemed
   an exemplary dystopia:
   a feature of the planet
   with no redeeming ones.

Objectionable to us is the conception
of an evil dwarf, evil because a dwarf,
   irrevocably stigmatized
   and demonized by shape. But this
was the old monstrosity shop of horrors,
   *noir* and foundered fairy tale:
   road movie, oriental quest,
   tragic show-down, comedy *shtik,*
   and waxworks ...

Yet didn't his author humanize him too
    with the weirdly loyal boy, Tom Scott,
who fought him and fought *for* him?
And with Daniel sleeping like a child
    on the table in the counting-house?

And didn't he make so distantly
reverberating a dark creation
    as to spring to the lips of scientists
bringing to book the Antarctic Peninsula?

        *KIT WRIGHT*

# The Conjuror

A small man silhouetted at the window
gestures along a gallery where the future
has gathered its faces, high above the Ghost's Walk
at Rockingham. His smile begins to conjure
sunlight from November, a perfumed present
out of blacking, silk from rags. He should be writing,

but 'Rhia Rhama Rhoos' knows even writing
is a stage, a model theatre, a Ghost's Walk
for characters that glide into the present
and turn to coins and cheers before the window
curtain closes. He is here today to conjure
away all fears, steam-powered by a future

that boils in him. But the shades of Past and Future
are nothing to the one that stalks his writing,
rattling its chains and ledgers at his window
with chilling deadlines – the laughing, joking Present,
whose progress underneath him is the ghost's walk
that most disturbs his patter, crying: 'Conjure

a guinea-pig from a box of bran, conjure
plum-pudding from an empty pan, present
the children with more sugar and a future
for your Aged P!' Hey Presto! there is writing
in the mist – it is a girl's name – on the window
that looks down to the yew-shapes of the Ghost's Walk,

where every mirrored year has heard the ghosts walk
whom Lady Dedlock watches from her window,
those blue slips passing. He dips his wand to conjure
estuarial dreams. Tosses them to a future
of cooling towers, warmth, flight. *If I were writing
a history of my life, I should make present* –
he preens his inky goose-quill – *ever-present*

*one face no Hamley's magnetist could conjure,*
*no necromancer stir, whose glance turns writing*
*to putrid city fumes, words to a Ghost's Walk,*
*poetry cold. I should distract the future*
*(I hold this vanished watch up to its window)*

*with one presence, one name, unhood a future*
*where righting something lights for good the Ghost's Walk*
*and conjures clean air through that leaded window.*

JOHN GREENING

# Royal Wedding Boxes

'I behold a long row of new square brick boxes set upon
damp clay, drained on an old and very bad system.'
*Household Words*

*1 Layette*

Clay is the word and clay is the flesh:
clay also the baked tablets which tell
how clay created the brick god Kulla;
how mother goddess, Queen Belet-ili,
was sung as 'Our Brick of Lapis Lazuli';
how bricks still bear a dimpled impress
as if touched by the curve of her belly.

*2 Boxes*

Downtrodden as brick-clay he treads,
its pit a nursery of treaders' gangrene,
the violent brickmaker in *Bleak House*
can't read the baby-books he's given.
Dickens, pressed for copy, will hit on
the bricklayer he watches wall gardens
and he thinks Irish, as thick as a brick.

*3 Reluctant Union*

Americans called it 'Irish Confetti',
half-bricks showering on nativists,
cops, Union Army draft enforcers
when the marriage was still young.
Differences rose at the reception;
the in-laws tired, poor, wretched,
arriving in coffin-ships not surreys.

*4 'My brother's name is Babylon ... '*

Clay grown tall patrols Route Irish,
watching children mould their clay
into what seem unmanned drones,
but are birds like those Jesus made
in the Infancy Gospel of St Thomas,
the Gospel inspiring many folksongs,
the Gospel where Jesus kills children.

*IAN DUHIG*

# Dickens: A Daydream

The scrapman's son bangs at our door,
skives school, like father, his before,
all crammed in van's hum. 'Anything, sir?'
curls wild, your scavenging people.

The doe-eyed girl at the café till
is child's height, yet does not spill
one bean from heaped trays, hammers bills,
your frantic, stunted people.

Bad teeth, bent hips, the pitbull's snarl
called you out from the lawyer's yarns.
Happiness bored you most of all,
white tables, good, quiet people.

One was your wife. You glimpsed ahead
the young actress's breasts instead,
buds crushed by silk. She never said
your name, changed dates, fooled people.

London, in its lost party time,
the trees' lit snow, the towers' gold chime,
the heat of bars, the twist of lime,
you shun as in a fever.

We meet beneath the dripping bridge,
soot, fear and sorrow on each ledge.
Hurt child, you scour each rag-strewn beach,
walk all night, stride and shiver

until the dawn strikes London's walls
and clangs Good morning from St Paul's.
Waitresses, Poles, striped bankers pour,
your million words. Sleep, river.

*ALISON BRACKENBURY*

# Ready Availability

The Bachelor the Bachelor the Barnacles the Bachelor the Badger
Dedlock (Dartle)(Drummle)(Duff) Cripples (Crimple)(Crupp)
Cupcake (Caught) Creakle (Gradgrind)(Grimwig) (Gulpage)(Great)
Rokesmith (Rudge)(Rudge)(Rudge)(Rudge)(Real)(Rug)
Sloppy (Slowboy)(Slightboy)(Slammer) Situation (Speculative)
   (Slight)
the Warden the Warden (Wardle)(Wardle)(Waterbrook)
Wopsle (clerk)(friend)(actor) (thesp.)(fame) (luck)
Plornish (plasterer)(lime) (aggregate)(hair)(lath fix)(shrinkage)
   (scuttlebuck)
Petowker Price Prigg Pross (pretty) (fix)(sort)(guess)
Podsnap Pogram (shuffle)(shard) Potterson (experience)(list)
start somewhere (Adams) rattle hiss wish concentrate realign
rhestr reallocate random rip retaliate render rich realise reach
Fanny Cleaver aka Jenny Wren cripple doll driven dressmaker
Dilber distrust Dodson and Fogg duplicity dealers (foxed)(slight
Scuffing)(rusted staples)(binding loose)(rip)
(uncut)(pages mssng) (water damage) (author sig)
(brittle)(buggered)(book club ed)(dedication "my Johnny lad
   you are
a wonderful boy, love Uncle Ron")(shelf cocked)(tanning visible)
(torn)(rip) (crease)(cracked)(defaced) (mild mould) (binding undone)
bought Grewgious guardian (Rosa Bud) man of many angles
no conversation (Fips) (Fish)(Finching) found (fell) (filched)
   (fractured)(fresh)(filled)(fixed)(frozen)(finished)
Pickwick eminence (see 7 above) mender of roads
filibuster final finisher surface like a calm pond (shouting)
storm at sea episodic (multiple) cliffhang forthright
(available) read (read to) don't stop.

*PETER FINCH*

# The Boys

reading *Barnaby Rudge*

She recognises this. The widow toiling
wearily along, while the boy *yielding*
*to inconstant impulse* is *darting,*
*flying, lingering. These were his delights*
and *she would not have abated them*
*by one sad word or murmur.*

These boys. Joe sits on his hands, *mumchance,*
– no future but being ordered about;
ravenous Hugh, *set loose* when his mother
broke the law, nurtures dark appetites
in his hidden corner, while Tappertit
snarls *I will be famous yet.*

She thinks of carrot-topped Callum's cackle
of a laugh, cruising into class with his
Porn Star badge, who died in Helmand,
Or doe-eyed Rob – no longer free to stare
out afternoons – who drove into a truck
one month after his sister died.

Or this boy, his low slung pants defying
gravity, his uniform of cool failing
to disguise the anxious eye-darts he flings
about him, telling his young friend. *Don't brag.*
He speaks more softly. *Karma is a bitch.*
*She's going to bite your ass.*

> TIM DOOLEY

# Realism

Nature was boring. Flowers went unnamed,
streams, he wrote, sparkled, and always a soft breeze blew.
But back in town he'd tramp all night through grimed
habitats from Parliament Fields to Kew,
or the miles from Kensal Green to Greenwich, watchful
as a botanist whose wondering eye is on
new, nondescript phyla. 'He knew it all'
his foot-sore friend marvelled, who'd thought *he* knew London.

And the voices! Pub songs, street cries, stage distress,
the pulpit vowels proclaiming good must die
like love and pretty babes. You want to cry
with laughter, Wilde remarked, at such excess.
But Carker, Merdle, Drummle, Fledgeby, mean
business. Money-tongued selachian gentlemen, they're
actual as the Thames or Jo's despair
at shit-slimed streets he knows he can't keep clean.

It's left to Jaggers, scrubbing with scented soap
hands that will never lose the stink of gaol,
to go from Newgate to dinner carrying hope
like portable property that's not for sale.

*JOHN LUCAS*

NOTE: The friend was George Augustus Sala, journalist, novelist,
and book-illustrator, who accompanied Dickens on many of his
nighttime walks across London.

# Goroo

"'Oh, my lungs and liver, what do you want? Oh, goroo, goroo!"
I was so much dismayed by these words, and particularly by
the repetition of the last unknown one, which was a kind of
rattle in his throat, that I could make no answer.
"Oh – goroo! – how much for the jacket?"
"Half-a-crown," I answered, recovering myself.
"Oh, my lungs and liver," cried the old man, "no! Oh, my eyes, no!
Oh, my limbs, no! Eighteenpence. Goroo!"
Every time he uttered this ejaculation, his eyes seemed to be
in danger of starting out'
*David Copperfield*

1

I have myself uttered such sounds as *goroo* when
the phlegm rose in me and my savage indignation
blew me purple. My lungs and liver were of no use,
nor my eyes that did verily start from their sockets.
Believe me, sir, it was no borborygmus but my fury.

So let me wind myself round my fit and fury
because what rises from the gorge or the sockets
of the eyes is a creature seeking to be of use,
and I have occasions, I assure you, for indignation
that cometh upon me, sir, just as and when.

2

It is injustice, sir, that lodges in my gut,
that and cheap jackets, cheap suits and all things cheap –
and we spit up cheapness, sir, indeed we do
and eyes and limbs are as nothing in the action,
are as foul fog in the lung or failure of liver.

What after all would you give me for these lungs, this liver?
What is the injustice that is a call to action?
Good Lord sir, we spit it up as we must and do.
And life is phlegm and savage, and this is a cheap
jacket, and, causes the deep *goroo* that rises from the gut.

3

And so it is eyes start from their sockets. Enough
the eye, or a pair of lungs. *Goroo goroo*
is a clearing of the throat which is connected
to the viscera in my kind. You'll know my kind
as you proceed on your way down the street.

I have the habitation of the street.
I take no delight, sir, in the kindness of the kind.
Eighteen pence and my gut are, I assure you, connected.
My rates of exchange are *goroo, goroo* and *goroo*.
Here is your jacket. Here's mine. Is that enough?

*GEORGE SZIRTES*

# Kite in 4.4 Time

> "'There's plenty of string,' said Mr. Dick, "and when it flies high,
> it takes the facts a long way.'"
> *David Copperfield*

for Niamh

Far up, beyond connections, see
the crimson diamond shiver and rise,

its streamer-hair, an oriflamme,
let out to fire the wintry sky.

This child has set her gauntlet, flier,
head to a headwind, face to the sky,

where bucked, inspired, it rides, outrides
the big wind's pushy phantom.

Her hand grips tight, catcradling sticky
skeins of string, winding the distance

in – then *giving* ... She'll take the height
in her stride as she runs to loose it again,

twitching a bell-pull, feeling it nudge
up, up, in chances of the wind,

until – too far – a slackness starts,
no coded gusts coming to hand,

and the lovely banner drifts, waylays,
dreams a moment in the air's intake,

then bolts, crosswise – she tries to dial
a love that's dead and can't reply.

Above, a red rag snaggled in the trees.
Nothing changed in the face of the sky.

*ANGELA LEIGHTON*

# Megalosaurus

' ... it would not be wonderful to meet a Megalosaurus,
forty feet long or so, waddling like an elephantine lizard
up Holborn Hill.'
*Bleak House* (1852)

Inkwell a primed black mirror
returning the day's greyness,
rain passes, fog settles, soot
lazes outside his barred window.

\*

Cobbles barely breach the mud
like worn down giants' teeth,
round-smoothed to flinty polish
by five million unwashed boots.

With squat massive quadrupedal
swagger through sliding mud,
slung belly scrapes cobble-tops
and horse dung in autumn fog,

implacable cold-blood omnibus
scaling diluvian Holburn Hill.
Talon-prints sunk in black mud
fill like tri-fold lakes. Thunder

rolls loud, dank London over
into lost Jurassic. Fern fronds
reflect from eyes as the lizard
snurf-snorts damp spit at mud.

\*

Good old Chuck, sat at his desk,
draws shutters on the beast,
allows soot and smog to fall outside,
returns to the blank page deadline.

His journalist's eye for *zeitgeist*,
he starts with the ghost, still muddled
from its Oxfordshire ossuary,
the novelty in his new novel.

*A. F. HARROLD*

# Even Supposing —

after *Bleak House*

Esther will have a little for herself.
I grope from bathroom to bed and smell
the dark. Outside, a coyote noses
the window where the bird hit. Feathers and
perhaps blood. Esther is
Esther Summerson, Dickens's sanguine
cloak. Duty is
the burden we would not give up. Noon,
blinds up, sun everywhere, the bird *would*
try to fly in to perch on the clock, to
the alarm's twitter and chirp.
Duty as cultivation, weed and tend.
A respect for seasons. Esther cups
compliments like bird's eggs. Gather and shine.
Morning, jasmine on the breeze, I raised
the blinds, slid one window behind the other,
half-screen, half-glass. Esther jingles
the housekeys, Esther tends. The coyotes stay
less in the field. Leaves scuttle.
The injured bird on the ground, I was due
elsewhere, I was due for some hesitation
mingled with fear. Esther
leaves her handkerchief, her initials where
she does not suspect
her mother will find them. When I returned,
the bird was gone. Duty and
grief: who will
set them aside, who will set them
in season? A little for herself.
In bed, I cannot see
the window glass: the coyote sniffs the room;
someone watches Esther
watch the stars.

CARRIE ETTER

# Approaches to Fog

*1 Bleak House*

            i

'Chance people on the bridges peeping
over the parapets into a nether sky of fog,
with fog all round them, as if they were
up in a balloon';

we meet them so early
these distant strangers
who cares who
they are?

            Fog makes the bleak oblique,
            deletes the intervening
            text. Hubbub silenced. Fog knows
            these first-page people
            aren't 'Chance'.

            ii

'He stood up to look over the parapet ... '

So close to the book's end now & right behind him,
watching at close-quarters, we're the bridge's
peeping Toms. Who'd have expected
this late on it was ourselves
we'd seen without knowing
back at the beginning
hazily through fog as
distant shapes,
'the black pit of water',
the 'flat lines of shore'
unprinting themselves?

'You don't know how wet and cold I am, [ ] how
many times I have lost my way in coming here
through [    ] thick fog.' 'A very foggy night,
with [     ] in the streets!' 'A man, sitting in [

  ] looked out of the fog.' 'A faint [           ]
inflamed and red through' [ ] 'night-fog, as
though it suffered [    ] like an eye'
'Some of the fog that hung about [    ]

seemed to have got into his throat; for he
spoke huskily, all' [    ] 'all muffled by [ ]
fog, indistinct to [ ] ear [ ] was every
object to the sight.'

'Almost reduced to [ ] groping
his [ ] hands (it [               ]
had grown so dark and the fog
had so much increased)'

he never once ceased [    ]
'I'll go when' [ ] 'you tell me'
'I'll go'
'Upon my word.'

*3 Bleak House*

'This is a London particular ... A fog, miss,'
'My dear Richard ... how CAN you say about nothing
particular?' 'I mean that it MAY be nothing
particular' '(there was no top or bottom in

particular)' 'beginning at the ends and bottoms
of the letters', 'dips down to the bottom
of his mind' 'at the bottom of all that goes
wrong in it', 'at the bottom of three fourths

of their troubles', 'the letters forming
the words', 'he put so many unnecessary letters
into short words that they sometimes quite
lost their English appearance'

'in an English stable', 'many an English
leaf or berry' 'growth of English soil'
'Ain't it English? Up!' 'Did you ever know
English law, or equity either,

plain and to the purpose?' 'It must be
English to someone, sir' 'intelligence
is weak in English' 'But before' 'But
before' 'But being' 'But business-

like' 'be particular to a word.'
'"A fog miss" said the young gentleman.'

*DAVID ANNWN*

# The Wrapped-Up Man

'My Lady Dedlock (who is childless), looking out in the early
twilight from her boudoir at a keeper's lodge, and seeing the
light of a fire upon the latticed panes, and smoke rising from
the chimney, and a child, chased by a woman, running out
into the rain to meet the shining figure of a wrapped-up man
coming through the gate, has been put quite out of temper.'
*Bleak House*

Wild to begin, the sky-blue paper folded
With his self-questionings like birds across it
Flying to their purposes and darkening
The page with their envisaged complications,
Birds with names like every lost ideal
Darkening, and still darkening, the sky,
He takes the pen and lets it slowly sip
The blue-black sour delivering ink.

From the twin windows of his brand-new study,
Where still in certain corners he swears he smells
Damp plaster, all he sees in the mirrored dripping
Unfamiliar vista from his Tavistock villa
Of a garden planted with his hopes, is rain.
A brand-new study and a brand-new book,
But rain fallen and falling, ancient as England.
The paper is folded, and he is folded in it.

And Tavistock House turns into Chesney Wold
And the pen flows over the page in his best blank prose
Like a dramatic chorus: 'The adjacent
Low-lying ground, for half a mile in breadth,
Is a stagnant river, with melancholy trees
For islands in it, and a surface punctured
All over, all day long, with falling rain.
My Lady Dedlock's "place" has been extremely dreary.

The weather, for many a day and night, has been
So wet that the trees seem wet through, and the soft
Loppings and prunings of the woodman's axe
Can make no crash or crackle as they fall.'
As the fog conceals, so the rain isolates.
It picks out glistening surfaces, like themes
In symphonies; like loneliness, regret,
And shame; emotions seeking their excuse.

And now he writes this cameo of welcome,
The labouring father, children at his knee
By the domestic hearth, the eager wife,
Borrowed from Thomson, or from Wordsworth, speaking
Clues which over his six-hundred pages
Will stand forever as an Eden not to be,
The phantom child, the man equally lost,
Wrapped up in law, and wrapped up in the plot.

He is the nameless one that she has lost
Through her ambition and her deadly pride
Where wedlock turns to deadlock in the rain.
How did he know it? Where did the image come from?
What insight does it take to disappear
Into your text? What heaviness
Of heart loads down the pen? Where is the love
That bursts beneath it, like a signature?

His words are elegy. The rain is tears.
Her childlessness a lie, and her love lost
Like her even temper, lost beyond bringing back.
And as he writes (as fast as any lawyer's clerk)
A smile crosses his face. He is Honoria,
Destined to die of terror and her conscience.
He is the cause and offspring of her love.
He is Esther. He is Hawdon. He is that gleaming parcel.

*JOHN FULLER*

# Boythorn's Garden

'sculpted' from *Bleak House*

a venerable wall
        with a ripened look

the old lime walk
        like green cloisters

the very shadows
        heavy with fruit

gooseberry bushes laden
    their branches arched
        rested on the earth

strawberries and raspberries

peaches basked by the hundred on the wall

spread nets and glass frames
    sparkling and winking
        in the sun

heaps of drooping pods
    marrows and cucumbers

every foot of ground
    a vegetable treasury

sweet herbs, all kinds of wholesome growth

(to say nothing of the neighbouring meadows
    where the hay was still carrying)

the air a great nosegay

the feathers hung in garlands
    to scare the birds
        hardly stirred

the wall had such a ripening influence
    that where, here and there, high up,
        a disused nail and scrap of list
            still clung to it

easy to fancy they had mellowed
    with the changing seasons

rusted and decayed
    according to the common fate

*MONIZA ALVI*

# The Consolation of Walls

'I hope he found some consolation in walls. I almost think he did.'
*Bleak House*

There is a wall inside me against which
I have been kicking a small rubber ball
                                    For years.

Sometimes it rolls back flat along the ground.
Sometimes it bounces back like feelings plotted
                                    On a graph,

That old oscillation of up and down.
I can't decide if it's the motive force
                                    Of ball

Bouncing against wall I feel in feeling
Or if it's the stoical resistance
                                    Of that

Stonewall part of me that never submits.
And which is better, moving ball or wall?
                                    For now,

Like poor Mr Jellyby, I'll settle for
The cool consolation of a wall against
                                    My brow.

The ball can rest inside me like a stone,
As hard and rubbery as death, unkicked,
                                    Unthrown.

*TERRY CREE*

# Merrylegs

homage to *Hard Times*

Mr Ruskin senior, purveyor of sherry 'Poeticall',
grand tourist and most hard-working Pa,
even he thought tales could show us naught
but *vain loves and fruitless deaths*.

So teach 'em not, M'Choakumchild,
a lost dog is a lost dog: Fact.
But it scampers on, past the palazzo
of Murray's Mill, down Back China Lane

and the undercrofts of those lint-specked, fruitless deaths,
a little, panting circus dog who will run rings
round Bounderby and take poor Gradgrind
from the life he thought he led into a tale

of his own manufacture where his children
he devours, and too late repents it –
vain his love for them. All these Merrylegs,
*the learned dog*, leaves with us and is away.

*JEFFREY WAINWRIGHT*

# Hard Times

This is what the rain has brought me:
snails, slugs, the slow blur of past summers.
My long skirts are conducting their movements,
caught in an inching, the twist of a shell.

I could sing in this rain if you would allow it.
For who in their right mind could hold weather against me,
who in the universe refuse me this:
being able to stand with my face to the sky?

The house let in water, denying edges.
The gutters overflow.
What place is this where I become
a blade of grass, a tree?

Because my feet are rooted in the earth I grow.

*DERYN REES-JONES*

# Traps

'We were at the foot of the American Fall. I could see an
immense torrent of water tearing headlong down from
some great height, but had no idea of shape, or situation,
or anything but vague immensity.'
*American Notes* (1842)

Why should Marseilles be
so strange as a set-
piece opening for
that novel? *Little
Dorrit*'s weather, names
and places all seem
diverted in the
first paragraph. I'm
lost already. Did
he get there? How did
he get there? Look it
up.
    So don't expect
London, railways, fog
or some industrial
waste. Hoping for cash
at the start, estates
or some other power-
space of an England
satisfactorily
gone astray or left
behind in a trap.
Tell time-travelling?
Those means of movement
studiously loved,
evoked, clip-clop, or
steam, demolition,
mapping out hot wet
gowns and stuffing, that

smelly leather shined
up from the slaughter-
house. Stench of headlong
destination – get
there in a week and
it's reduced to juicy
meat, boiling up
for circulation
in any head or
blood-flow or nervous
whiplash in the dark.

There now. Think of the
luxury or pain
of staring – over
and over: 'stared' three
times, 'staring' seven –
in those first few lines.
What an impression,
what an announcement
(eighteen fifty-seven)
of what might now be
judged Po-Mo playful
creativity:
just look at, and look
back, and be looked at.
Staring. The sun'll
get you. It knows what
it's looking for.
                    Though
I'm also stuck (can't
think it through) with young
Dickens' Buffalo
to Niagara
train trip, not knowing
what he would hear or
see till the carriage

door opened and there
was the roar of some
place invisible.
What's waiting's in charge
I think. 'No idea.'

*JON GLOVER*

# Dickens Discovers His Italian Babylon

In the course of two months
the flitting shapes and shadows
of my dismal entering reverie
gradually resolved themselves
into familiar forms and substances

and I already began to think
that when the time should come
for closing the long holiday
and turning back to England
I might part from Genoa with

anything but a glad heart.
It is a place that *grows upon you*
every day. There seems to be
always something to find out.
There are the most extraordinary

alleys and by-ways to walk about in.
You can lose your way (what a comfort
that is, when you are idle!) twenty
times a day. It abounds in
the strangest contrasts:

things picturesque, ugly, mean,
magnificent, delightful and offensive
break upon the view at every turn.
The houses are immensely high
painted in all sorts of colours

and are in every stage of damage,
dirt and lack of repair.
As it is impossible for coaches
to penetrate into these streets
there are sedan chairs, gilded

and otherwise, for hire in divers
places. I had earlier made
the mistake of asking the whip
to take me to Piazza San Bernardo.
The young women are not generally
pretty but they walk remarkably well.
I had earlier made the mistake
of asking the whip to take me
to an apothecary. The women are not
generally pretty but oh they walk

remarkably well. And how shall I forget
the Streets of Palaces: Strada Nuova
and Via Balbi!: the great, heavy, stone
balconies, one above another, and
tier over tier: with here and there,
one larger than the rest, towering
high up – a huge marble platform;

the doorless vestibules, massively
barred lower windows, immense
public staircases, thick marble pillars,
strong dungeon-like arches, and
dreary, dreaming, echoing vaulted
chambers: among which the eye
wanders again, and again, and again
as every palace is succeeded by another
– the terrace gardens between house
and house, with green arches of
the vine, and groves of orange trees
and blushing oleander in full bloom
twenty, thirty, forty feet above

the street. The steep up-hill streets
of small palaces with marble terraces
looking down into close by-ways –
the magnificent and innumerable

churches; and the rapid passage
from a street of stately edifices
into a maze of the vilest squalor,
steaming with unwholesome stenches
and swarming with half-naked
children and whole worlds of
dirty people – make up, altogether,
such a scene of wonder: so lively
and yet so dead: so noisy and yet
so quiet: so obtrusive, and yet
so shy and lowering: so wide awake
and yet so fast asleep: that is
a sort of intoxication to a stranger
to walk on, and on, and on, and
look about him. A bewildering
phantasmagoria, with all the
inconsistency of a dream and all
the pain and all the pleasure
of an extravagant reality!

I made the mistake of asking
the whip to take me
to Vico dell'Amor Perfetto.
The women are not generally
pretty but oh but oh they
do walk remarkably well.

*JULIAN STANNARD*

# Marshalsea Quadrille

1

Debts stacked up like bricks
at the Tabard as I lay,
watching a chink of sky
from the slushy sticks

the Surrey side of the Thames.
Debts stacked up like bricks,
and sundry heretics
and smugglers came to terms

but the pauper's room cost double
when the gaoler threw a six.
Debts stacked up like bricks,
the bricks stacked up like trouble

and toppled on the pricks
who'd have chucked them back (fair's fair)
if they'd not been starving where
debts stacked up like bricks.

2

At the Tabard as I lay,
saving for my salvation,
the criminal population
tripled in a day.

I counted out my cash
at the Tabard as I lay
and then it rolled away.
I heard a distant splash,

but, loaded, didn't care
what load I couldn't pay
at the Tabard as I lay
and prayed some good soul there

would buy my round-e-lay,
and underneath the tap
would thrust his little cap
at the Tabard as I lay.

3

Watching a chink of sky
he passes Nancy's Stairs,
not knowing they'll be hers –
only that good souls die

un-saved by gilded towers,
watching a chink of sky.
He gulps a ha'penny pie
with a few fanciful tears.

Some grubby gargoyles that
might be debating why
watching a chink of sky
concerns this sewer-rat

jeer as he scuttles by.
To Lant Street, then, and home –
contented in the gloom,
watching a chink of sky.

4

From the slushy sticks,
a London Particular
snuffs Perpendicular
to smoking wicks.

He often walks all night.
from the slushy sticks,
to skin his cicatrix,
his blister-pack of light,

and save the child who drowned
although he'd learned some tricks
from the slushy sticks –
the child who won't be found

by any politics
or power that snivels pity,
but never walked to the city
from the slushy sticks.

*CAROL RUMENS*

# Costume Drama

'his ventures had been utterly reckless'
*Little Dorrit*

Under their broad bacchanalian ceiling,
a film company moved in its canopied bed
for the death scene, but of whom?

False shutters were tacked over windows,
a reprobate gentleman dunned for debt.
They had placed tall white candles
by mirrors in that makeshift bedroom
for a theatrical gloom.

They had built themselves a pontoon bridge
to track from the Temple of Venus
across lake water to a stately pleasure dome,
a fictional Venice forbidden us ...

Around the lake, stray extras roamed.
Duckweed rafts were shooting a sluice.
It was like the shady bathtub end
of a banker, a banker with annual bonus
– or so I imagined.

*PETER ROBINSON*

# Until

1

You look down, far down, into the past
as though you sat on a balcony like
Amy Dorrit above the Grand Canal
and saw the water drain away like years

until 'realities' remained. At last
you will be able, at long last, to track
how things took shape and who you are, unpick all
fictions or versions until truth appears,

or till you sense that that can never happen.

2

You lean into the stairwell of your choices,
and glimpse at best a profile's angled hurry.

Ears strained, you might just catch a medley
of jumbled voices.
                    And then a door thuds shut
on the whole rickety structure. *You have to let go*

you tell yourself, holding the banister rail
so tightly that your knuckles whiten.

*MICHAEL O'NEILL*

# Sensation

'... say that my answer was, RECALLED TO LIFE.'
*A Tale of Two Cities*

Two nights, two roads, two hills,
two reeking fogs, two passageways
dimly lit, two persons.

Among those terrors concealed
in the darkness something golden,
something *blazing strange.*

Awake by a small fire, a person
interviewing himself. Across
in the darkness, a truth revealed.

Two fires lit on a foreshore,
the shore stretching only as far
as the fires allow. Two men.

Rowing in from the darkness, a man
or a man and a boy or a young man alone.
A small fire. In sight, two persons.

*JANE DRAYCOTT*

# My Heart and My Liver

*Magwitch, Great Expectations*

Marsh gas, smoke, slant rain from the East
rattles a pattern of print onto paper,
sweeps river to flux, an eel of a story that opens
London like a book, terror and promise
there in the *small bundle of shivers*
that made me, a child, fear the very same he
who might softly creep and creep his way
and tear me open, or that very same he
who lamed by stones, cut by flints,
was stung by nettles, the very same way
this reader now, grown, awoken, gazing
at the marsh, *just a long black horizontal line*
and the river *just another horizontal line*
feels all those words, line upon line,
enter a grateful, hungry, unreconciled heart.

MAURA DOOLEY

# Little Clouds

A boy at his bedroom window,
in the morning, doing breathing exercises,
the window is open and he is drawing in air,
like a swimmer, his hands pressed against
his narrow chest and he inhales deeply
and slowly, making sure to hold his breath
momentarily and then exhaling slowly.
The scene before him has not changed
since he moved to his grandmother's house
with his mother and sister several years before,
when he was little more than a boy.
Now he is turning into adolescence
and the doctor has recommended these
morning and last thing at night exercises
to help him overcome the asthma attacks,
which afflict him from time to time.
The yard is long and narrow;
at the far end by the back door
there is a coalbunker and an outdoor lavatory.
At the pantry door stands a wire mesh larder
and next to it an old mangle
for draining off excess water
from the washing before it was hung up
on the line to dry on Mondays.
It's rarely used. The laundry is collected
on Wednesdays and delivered on Fridays.
The milkman calls every day before the house stirs.
The evening paper comes in just before six at night.
The piano is tuned by a blind man
who appears each autumn, the hedges cut
by a bald-headed Magwitch in spring;
the house painted and decorated by Mr. Wright,
the insurance man collects his premium Saturday nights.
At the beginning, a gas lighter popped
the street lamps on the pavement outside.

Beyond the yard on the left is a row of houses,
the backs of which – kitchens, bathrooms,
landing windows and gardens, run behind an entry
that leads into a derelict site and the backs
of more houses. Above this network of houses
the streets rise into the chimneys of other houses,
the sloping roofs, the telegraph poles, the bright sky.
He breathes again deeply and looks out,
not really seeing anything beyond the wall
of the landing and the spangled glass
of the bathroom window.
The red brick of the house next door
glows a little in the morning light.
There is barely a breeze but little clouds
carry across the view. He closes the window carefully
and turns back into his room.
Above his bed are pictures of motorcycles,
the fireplace is empty and the large wardrobe
next to it reflects the young man
in the shadow of his room. The dressing table
and the shelves in the nook of the chimneybreast
are sparse of ornament. His dressing gown hangs
on the back of the closed door.
He looks absent-mindedly at himself
in the long mirror of the wardrobe,
pulls on his shoes and leaves the room
to the sound of a couple of children
running down the back lane, shouting
and teasing one another. The rooms
at the back of the house are in the shade
where the grandfather clock on the landing
strikes twelve. And then again.

*GERALD DAWE*

# I Am Greatly Changed

*Great Expectations*

That poor dream, as I once used to call it,
has all gone by. (The freshness of beauty
is the saddened softened light
of once proud eyes.) I have very often – .

I intended to come back. Tracing, proving.
I thought – . I thought you would like – .
'God bless you, God forgive you!'
you said to me.

I am greatly changed.
I thought you would like to shake hands.
What I had never felt before
was the friendly touch.

I very often hoped – .
I have often
thought of you.
An imaginary case.

I have been considerate and good,
I have been bent and broken,
suffering, God forgive you.
Suffering, God bless you.

(Suffering has been stronger
than all other teaching,
a heart to understand
what my heart used to be.)

The ground belongs!
Everything else,
little by little, has gone.
I wonder you know me.

If you could say to me then
'God bless you! God forgive you!'
you will not hesitate now.
('God bless you,' you said to me).

Poor, poor old place!
Ruined place.
Would I step back?
Ignorant, held?

She gave me her assurance
(her voice, her touch).
I took her hand,
evening mists rising now, tranquil.

'We are friends.'

*RICHARD PRICE*

# Orlick's Devil

'When I was small and timid, he gave me to understand
that the Devil lived in a black corner of the forge'
*Great Expectations*

The devil is a journeyman
The devil wants a holiday
The devil is a surly 'un
The devil dogs you every day

The devil's job is on the line
The devil's in his cups again
The devil says what's yours is mine
The devil lurks on Lover's Lane

The devil lives inside the forge
The devil breathes on stale air
The devil rises at your gorge
The devil's foot is on the stair

The devil nurses every shame
The devil knows you for a liar
The devil's waiting in the flame
The devil in the lime-kiln fire

The devil never laughed or smiled
The devil only learned to smirk
The devil never was a child
The devil always had to work

The devil likes to shower sparks
The devil forges links of chain
The devil hammers shrews and larks
On the anvil in your brain

ADRIAN BLAMIRES

# Havisham à la Mode

No one has got it, so to satisfy my critics:
it is really all about the dress.
Few brides can wear theirs thirty years on
without stinking of cedar.

Theirs lie tissued like my untouched shoe,
but I can fasten pearl buttons
every day, if I choose.

No feeding family, no babies have pushed me
out of shape and it's surprising
how lasting wedding cake can be.

It's all about my silk-and-lace cocoon,
a second skin skimming my bones.
I love its yellowed ivory
resisting time and laundry for a look,
a shimmer in narrow light beams.

Here's a tip – stay out of the sun.
Shadow and a well-draped veil
show complexion best, will give you skin
pale and papery as moon moth.

I may have overdone this.
I don't look good naked.

*KATE NOAKES*

# In Their Manner of Speaking

Directions towards a performance in mime of *Our Mutual Friend*

*(The characters are all present on a dark stage. They perform
only when spot-lit, sometimes solo, sometimes in duets or trios,
in various permutations which possibly re-plot the novel)*

*Eugene Wrayburn* leaning back with a heavy sigh, drowsily
*Lizzie Hexam* mournfully opening her eyes to look on the
    ground
*Bella Wilfer* eyelids drooping, coldly tossing her curls
*Mrs Wilfer* adjusts the handkerchief under her chin, resignedly
*John Rokesmith/Harmon* with a glance and a half-smile, gently
*Wrayburn* arms folded, disparaging, eyes shut, enjoying his
    cigar
*Silas Wegg* musing, nodding with an air of gentle resignation
*Noddy Boffin* smiling, left arm nursing his knotted stick
*Wegg* bestirring himself to take precaution, feelingly, sulkily
*Boffin* leans forward with confidential dignity, alarmed appeal
*Mrs Boffin* smoothing her dress with an air of immense
    enjoyment
*John* with an air of reluctance, deference, earnestness, hesitating
*Bella* with a little stamp of her foot, pointing her forefinger
    merrily
*Mrs W* with a dignified bend of her head, with an indignant
    shiver
*Wegg* one arm a-kimbo, with modesty, with increasing
    complacency
*Boffin* one hand to his chin, crumpling a blotted note in the other
*Mrs B* clapping hands, gaily rocking to and fro, laying aside her
    shawl
*John* with a quick turn, correcting himself, perfectly composed,
    soothing
*Wrayburn* with the air of a philosopher lecturing a disciple,
    vexedly
*Rogue Riderhood* fumbling with an old sodden fur cap, with
    a leer

*Lizzie* in some confusion, as a recollection flashes upon her
*Wegg* as if beginning to regard himself in quite a new light
*Boffin* takes a piece of chalk from his pocket, abstractedly
*Wrayburn* plaintive, with gravity, perplexed, inquisitive
*Riderhood* shading his mouth with his hand, ducking,
    with a servile air
*Bradley Headstone* with pale and quivering lips, eyes averted
*Lizzie* with hands now covering her anxious face, with starting
    tears
*Jenny Wren* screws up her eyes and chin, looks prodigiously
    knowing
*Bella* as if italicising with a twist of dimpled chin, energetically
*Boffin* wiping his mouth with an air of much refreshment
*John* forming the syllables of the word 'nonsense' on his lips
*Headstone* wiping the starting perspiration from his face,
    despairingly
*Jenny* with an angry little shake of her right fist close before
    her eyes
*Headstone* shakes from head to foot, with a clutch at the breast
    of his shirt
*Bella* looks comically frightened, with childish gravity
*Rumty Wilfer* with his hand to his eyes, dubiously, mildly
*Jenny* looking through her screwed-up fist like an opera glass
*Headstone* protesting with errant hands, in a half-suffocated way
*Jenny* holds out her hand, looking upward, her needle pricking
    the air
*Wegg* nodding with an air of friendly recognition, condoling
*Boffin* with a glance of discomfiture, rubbing his ear
*Mrs B* with left hand thoughtfully touching her brow, placidly
*Bella* lays the forefinger of her glove on her lip
*John* patient but proud, looking steadily, with beaming face
*Mrs W* apostrophises the air with scornful fortitude, sublime
    severity
*Rumty* apologetic, his hand enjoining patience, with trepidation
*Wegg* cheering up bravely, slowly, knowingly, exasperated
*Riderhood* beats his open right hand on the palm of his left
*Headstone* folding his hands before him, unfolding them

*Lizzie* with indignation she cannot repress, raising her eyes
*Wrayburn* with determination, calmest indifference, contrition
*Wegg* nodding with an air of insinuating frankness
*Boffin* staring at the moon, with commiseration, a little staggered
*Bella* with eyes looking away, slaps herself with her glove
*John* excitedly, joyfully, fondly, coaxingly, laughing outright
*Rumty* meditating, stoutly, cherubically, approvingly
*Mrs W* assuming a deadly cheerfulness, an awful air of politeness
*Mrs B* draws a long breath, laughs with childlike glee
*Headstone* with a lumbering show of ease, stolid, vacant, self-communing
*Riderhood* knuckling his forehead, backing a little, snapping his fingers
*Lizzie* with an incredulous smile, with a look of supplication
*Wrayburn* again folding his arms, candidly, as if he were a little stung
*Headstone* trying to constrain his working mouth, with a stab at the sky
*Riderhood* smiting his right leg, head aslant, stubbornly chewing
*Wrayburn* with a look of appeal, indecision, rallying
*Lizzie* trembling, resolute
*John* keeping his countenance, interrogatively
*Bella* turning suddenly, putting out her right foot, with a loving laugh
*Boffin* wrinkling his face into a map of curves and corners
*Rumty* with a flagrant assumption of unconsciousness

ALAN HALSEY


NOTE: *Our Mutual Friend* concerns itself in various ways with
literacy and legibility. 'All print is shut to me,' laments Boffin;
he and several other characters would have no access to the
speeches Dickens attributes to them – their spoken words have in
effect been taken away and hidden from them. Suppose, then, that
speech were removed from the novel and we were granted only
Dickens's accounts of his characters' *manners* of speaking – then we
have mime and we have stepped into that popular drama Dickens so

loved. Mime is nevertheless a conscious demonstration that
the gulf between gesture and its description, whether or not shut
in print, belongs to a different order of legibility, briefly touched
upon in Wrayburn's remarks on 'that very word, Reading, in its
critical use'. The extent to which the characters in *Our Mutual Friend*
are illegible to each other is in part due to their levels
of literacy – and yet, in great part, not.

# A Short History of the Decline and Fall of the Roman Empire

culled from the Works of the Honourable Edward Gibbon
Deceased by Silas Wegg Esquire, Vendor of Ballads

The times for more than four score years and ten, when Hadrian,
The emperor who built our eternal Scottish wall,
Trajan, Nerva and two Antonines ruled, were halcyon.
Then came a woeful, long Decline and at last the Fall.

Commodus, whose great sire fought and philosophised,
Began the tale. Heedless and of unsound mind,
In the arena with gladiators he exercised
And then he was strangled like many of his kind.

Government was restored until Elagabalus.
His uncle, crowned close to the Caledonian border,
Could not conceive a nephew of vice so fabulous
I cannot name out of respect for public order.

The Decline progressed despite souls won for Christianity.
Of their holy martyrdoms I would wax lyrical
A consequence of which is your kind humanity
Though Mr. Gibbon's narrative is somewhat satirical.

Almost the last of rulers in the West was Honorius
Who mistook great Rome for one of his chickens.
An emperor more absurd and inglorious
Could not be invented even by Mr. Charles Dickens.

In the East the second Rome, Constantinople,
Throve a thousand years with the laws of Justinian,
Which in tomes inlaid with ruby, sapphire, opal
Survive to still confound learned opinion.

Office and place abounded; eunuch, protosebastocrator,
Gold! Gold! the cruel empress Irene, the Bulgar slayer Basil,
Much like the Turk whom I will mention later,
I am, sirs, bewildered by their dizzy dazzle.

Yet Decline continued and the empire's confines dwindled
So the Turk laid siege to the second Rome where distrust
Not emperors ruled, where no Roman valour kindled,
The last Constantine slain and lost beneath a heap of dust.

This gentle ladies and gentle men is my humble abstract
Perused from the Honourable Gibbon by Silas Wegg
To stimulate your pursuit of historical fact
And a few pence for a much put-upon person with one leg.

*JAMES SUTHERLAND-SMITH*

# Rubbish Theory

'By which he probably meant that his mind would have been
shattered into pieces without this fiction of an occupation.'
*Our Mutual Friend*

1

Now they're carting away the dust-heaps
on an earthmover and truck –
the pulverized halls impacted with work,
ink, tears and perspiration.
Hurrying through a quintessence of dust
blown into eyes and face,
I'll ghost past disturbance in the trees'
flustered rustling at winter's end.
The dust-heaps catch what light there is
on a day rain-bearing wind
gusts remnant leaves about the place
and taking the register, ticking all boxes,
mind, I'll pay my way
with this fiction of an occupation ...
Year on year,
I'll be guessing who those characters are
or dropping into poetry
despite each sudden blast, each blight;
now the dust-heaps disappear.

2

Streets are paved with takeaway
wrappers, strewn sheets, cans
and posters for elections ...
Attenuated traipsing figures
have their shadows stalking them,
each with a private memory
migrant to this point.

Sun sets on brick and greenery.
More distant figures come –
those that struggled to get here,
others who'd not made it
and you that have, uncertain eyes
at checkout till or queue.

3

From blue-grey rain-fronts cut with sun
one slant, mitigating ray
back-lights the whole equivocal scene.
A bus runs through old factory
dockland this late afternoon –
its slums of possibility,
olfactory traces quite gone in thin air.
The dusk glows over familial faces
and matter out of place is
glinting with a change of weather,
mind or heart, if chance would have it
and, no, we'll never, never, never ...
Love, we'll pay our way.

*PETER ROBINSON*

# Found in the River

Sometimes, approaching light
occurs beyond terraces, cranes,
the silvery distance
of the dredged-at sea.
Ducks bob and weave,
and the rest rots down
to pub talk, postcodes,
pads of matted weed.

From Rochester to Rotherhithe,
the river's urban bucolic:
intrusion, expulsion of tides
between warehouse developments,
bearded wooden piles,
they bring in, drag out
infertile salmon, stinging brine.

That man had just about enough.
Bewhiskered, posed at the tiller,
he takes the reach, his wife
and children arranged
on deck for the photo.
The boat he'd bought at Herne Bay;
London he'd read of in Dickens,
its backdrop's derricked outline.

Between these capital silhouettes,
I can just imagine
hawkers stalling outside his shop
or Veneerings peeled off
to chat at social functions.
He's sailed straight into a novel,
a saturated city.

Look back from a ferry nosing west
and it fits: the ill-judged passions,
fraternal rivalry, gist
of great-grandfather's plot.
Distracted by business,
by making ends meet,
he stands here taking stock
while Gaffer Hexham
punts out from the shore,
reaches down, collecting bodies,
and then pushes onwards, searching for more.

*TOM PHILLIPS*

# Thames Clippers

In these times of ours
   we take the Tate Boat
run by Thames Clippers –
   they count on the bodies –
friends, colleagues, utter
   strangers, men in suits
who might turn up
   to fix a copier ... Who are we then,
leaving our mud-lark
   prints on tidal sand under
the Festival Hall, along
   with rope-coils, tar blobs,
crushed *Fanta* cans?

Come dusk we glimpse
   the ghost-boat. Man and girl
heave on board the sacking.
   Weighs a ton. Old Fezziwig,
is it? Shallows flounder
   over his features. Colleagues,
men in suits, the two
   gentlemen, Stan, the ones
you were expecting, might
   turn up one day though
concerning the exact year
   there is no need to be precise.

Two figures. Autumn evening closing in.
   Between Southwark Bridge which is of iron
and London Bridge which is of stone.

*PETER CARPENTER*

# The Stolen Chapter

Between Southwark Bridge which is of iron
and London Bridge which is of stone
between the Gates of Tusk and the Gates of Horn
a dirty and disreputable boat

not a fisherman he had no net no hook no line
not a waterman a lighterman a river-carrier
the crazy boat had no appliance beyond
a rusty boathook and a coil of rope

allied to the river bottom rather than
its surface for the slime and ooze
that covered it its sodden state
they were seeking what they often sought

his eyes watched every little race
and eddy of the tide its arrowheads
against which the boat could scarce make headway
despite the girl pulling a pair of sculls

very easily but in her look
there was a touch of dread or horror
*Tide runs strong here. Keep her well afore*
*the sweep of it* the floating logs off wharves

obstructed the current the paddles of
the river steamboat beat the filthy water
and were obscured in the setting sun
a puddle at their feet like watery blood

the thing they had in tow would lunge itself
in an awful manner when the boat was checked
sometimes tried to wrench itself away
though mainly followed meekly in its wake

*JAMIE MCKENDRICK*

# The Figures

Between Southwark Bridge which is made of silver
and London Bridge which is made of gold,
they float and hover, the figures, through-composed
by night and rain, rowing against the working river,
its writhing surface roped and plied
like a fosse of underground cables.

The earth turns and a body appears.
A camera too revolves, a leather barque
sets out once more towards the North, arch
that bends the starry dome. The whole sector
is on fire: oil, corn and copper at all-time highs
above All Hallows Lane and Angel Passage.

Another boat there. Even at this depth
I hear it graze and grate the other's stern
as one mouth says: 'What world does a dead man
belong to?' to which a second mouth
responds: 'The Other World'. 'And to what world
does money belong?' But here the currents

bear me off again: a glitch, a stitch, a chrysalis
slowly unspooling, whose data-cloud
of flags and flitters, whose wandering shroud,
seems but the more diaphanous
for the echo-graph of numbers and names
that stream around and through it, systemic change

cascading past the glassy cliffs,
the gates of silver and the gates of gold,
where passionate shadows trawl the cold
incessantly, stoking it with aching wrist,
stripping the *fattie wave* to its bone,
invisible hands that root in my cake-hole.

*CONOR CARVILLE*

# Cold Case

*Edwin Drood to his Maker*

You bastard, you, to leave me thus.
I cannot even say for sure
that this is death; two hundred years'
purgatory of unkindness.

The outlook from here is a blank,
a nothing, a ceiling of lime
raging against my open eyes.
What I wouldn't give, once, to blink.

And there will be no confession
from opium-bed, witness-stand
or prison-cell. The bloody hand
will never chafe in penal chains.

And how for Rosa, my rose-bud,
to come to terms with the guilty
unpunished, the guiltless not free
and I possessed of breath nor blood?

Would that you were the proper death
of me. It's for the gutter-press
and gossips to conjecture, guess
what could have become of us both.

I will neither rise nor dissolve
nor lie at rest. So tell me, Boz,
how you'd make up your mind, because,
because I, I am unresolved.

*ANTONY DUNN*

# The Small Matter of A Bracelet

We don't know all about it,
but let's just suppose you bought Nelly
a gold-chain bracelet, padlock
shaped like a heart, not dissimilar
to one your wife has already,
as your imagination doesn't run much to gifts.

In this plot twist, the jeweller, absent-minded
or too lazy to check work-orders,
sends the piece to Gad's Hill Place. Wrong
as it turns out, the oldest mistake
in the book of *A Hundred Things
Not to Do When Having an Affair*.

Light blue touch paper. Stand well back. Look.
Catherine opens the gilt-tooled box.

Your explanation of custom,
presents for actresses in your plays,
falls on her you-must-think-me-stupid ears.
She's off. You're writing press releases
about *abominably false rumours.*
You really couldn't make this up.

*KATE NOAKES*

# Pip and Nell

I take the train to Slough and think of you:
First author of the child, first inky clerk
Of waif-lost, foot-slogged love. Here you kept dark
The truth of Nelly Ternan, eyes pool blue,
Eighteen and upward, one Estella true –
Ah, Mr Dick, King Charley, she leaves her mark
Upon your copy; hers the anvil spark
Of guilt that strikes you Modern through and through.
For suddenly your couple, Pip and Nell,
Flounder quite expectationless. Love's only
Ending evokes some never ending slough –
Or marsh – child sweethearts in a sexual hell
Stolen behind net curtains. How these lonely
Transports chill me: sweat from your wordsmith brow.

*DEREK BEAVEN*

NOTE: Dickens, under the pseudonym of Charles Tringham,
for a time kept his mistress, Ellen Ternan, in a small house
in Slough High Street.

# Graphic

It was just as Phiz would have sketched it: a horrid swirl
of smoke and smuts, spun wheels bent on etching themselves
into the soft turf of the mud-bank, at once tragic and picaresque

– perhaps a wrapper design for a racy romance, or a giveaway
scene too early on in the book: fiction must grip as it unfolds,
the author's grayscale rendered starkly in the reader's mind

by the artist's play of livid light, his oil-thick stippling. Pages
almost turn themselves, human figures hurry past, cross-hatched,
jacketless. Yes, there was a woman (no better than she should be,

by the tilt of her hat), a driver, stickler for timing, looking grim.
In one vignette, that flash of red flag glimpsed far too late to brake
(not hard to guess it's red); on the facing plate, a chiaroscuro

of soot and buckled iron. A parasol, its ribs and shredded silks.
And there, in the bottom left-hand gutter, a sheaf of leaves
you'd swear were still fluttering, a month of serials spilt in mid-plot.

*LESLEY SAUNDERS*

NOTE: Dickens, Ellen Ternan and her mother were returning
from France in May 1865 when they were involved in a train crash
on the viaduct near Staplehurst in Kent. 'And then, as he prepared
to take leave of the death scene, Dickens did a remarkable thing.
Remembering that his manuscript was still in the pocket of his
overcoat, he clambered back into the swaying carriage and
retrieved it.'

# The Crash

The Press represented him
offering water to a woman
stricken among the wreckage.

In his own account, 'Suddenly
we were derailed, beating the
ground like the car of a balloon

deflating.' Two ladies, his
fellow-passengers, cried out. He
urged calm and climbed out the window.

Later he wrote to Charing
Cross enquiring on behalf of
one of them about lost items –

a watch chain, a smaller chain,
a watch-key, all of these gold
including a seal inscribed 'Ellen'.

In Paris it was the jewel
scene in Gounod's new opera
had so distressed him – 'like the

echo of things in my own
heart.' She was Marguerite who had
borne and lost his child. He was Faust.

Or he was Manette released
from the Bastille of marriage
but only to secrecy and shoes.

He told Collins, 'Never was man
so seized and rendered by one
Spirit.' Coldly, his wife was banned

from the bedroom; finally from
home and family. 'My father',
Kate said, 'was like a madman.'

His son Charley met him walking
with her, 'the actress', on Hampstead
Heath. They passed without a word.

Hornpipe dancer, all-night walker,
joker, moralist and 'most
famous man in England', he gave

Lucie Manette Ellen's golden
hair and blue eyes, and something
interrogative in the brows.

Estella he gave that power
to make him love beyond reason,
and Bella Wilfer the same

strength softened by time. In a
postscript joke he told his readers
the Boffins, Lamles, Bella and

others, all 'in their manuscript
dress', had been with him in the
smashed carriage that lay on its side,

and when he had done what he
could to assist the injured, 'I
climbed back inside and rescued them'.

*

'You are part of my existence.
You have been in every prospect –
woods and water, cloud and sky.

'London's stones are not more real, nor
more impossible to dislodge.
Until my life's last hour, you

'cannot choose but remain a part.'
That was Pip to Estella –
but who was in his mind could so

invest it with passion if not
the lovely one in the wreckage
where lay the lost, the tell-tale gold?

    *C. K. STEAD*

# Passages

An after-breakfast brandy braces him
Against the *brise marine* – a mix of ozone, salt
And lavender on ladies' handkerchiefs
Waved at distant bathers' bobbing heads
And under these the whiff of fish-docks, decks
Awash with slime; scent he has sometimes caught
In plush Parisian *boudoirs* thronged with 'the sex' –
Each one for sale! – and on their unmade beds
In little shuttered rooms ... The morning packet,
Pennants fluttering and all its tackle trim,
Steams out and steers for Margate; young girls' griefs
Are not for days at Hardelot where John Hare
Walks towards him in a smoking jacket,
Laughing. *By Gar! Aha! Vat you tell me, Sare?*

\*

In the dark, in the cold
Of a frozen-fish container,
In a lorry or a hold,
Packed in tight, they lie
Trying not to cry.

Worth their weight in gold
To men all beard and belly
Who paid for them in cash,
Whose treasure-trash
Will be unpacked,
Shivering, fish-smelly,
At Portsmouth or Dover,
Who deal in hard fact
And harder blows,
In needles, in what grows
Hard and hot and red
Between the thighs
On a thin hard bed –

Their childhood is over.
From now on, threats, lies.
What could be plainer?

*

'The girls' who hang around outside 'Secrets' in the Gray's Inn Road
Stub their fag-ends in the overflowing ashtrays on chrome stands –
Miniatures of the floor-to-ceiling poles they gyrate around inside,
Flinging legs to flash shaved cunts at punters sitting on their hands
At tables, at the bar, in booths that have a whiff of chloride ...
They are from Lithuania, Czech, Ukraine; the Gray's Inn Road
Welcomes all, shrouds their secrets in a stale miasma
Of laws and lawlessness, of ash from ashtrays and ash-heaps,
Money and cigar-smoke and smoke from blackened chimneys
And the funnels of locomotives that chuffed through fields and spinneys
To Dover, Newhaven, thence to Boulogne, Dieppe and Paris –
To where one might forget about the girls thrown on the trash-heaps?

*ALAN JENKINS*

# Wandering in the Dark with Mr Dickens

*Customer*: Why is this pub called The Betsey Trotwood when
    it's miles from Kent?
*Barmaid*: They say she was a local madam – and Dickens lived
    nearby so he probably knew her …

Did you, as a midnight flâneur, meet her
on your ramblings when rain-rinsed streets were
sharp with darkened bricks, alleys, uneven stairs –
the other Betsey, who'd just popped out for air
while her girls snatched a fistful of sleep or
led their gentlemen to her battened door?

Did you find her at the refuge with your
lost women, hear their stories, see them claw
at chances (a tablecloth, the household crocks,
someone's watch) before a carriage to the docks
and dispatch to a colony? Did she
add strength to Miss Mary's gentility?

Did rumoured blows, or the handsome young rake
she paid off, inspire her character's new shape?
Did she long for a cottage on a cliff,
want to be a respected, seaside Miss
with only donkeys and pesky boys to try her?
Or was that barmaid another story teller?

    *ROBYN BOLAM*

# Dali on Dickens

Years from now, measured by a Dali clock,
Worn on a bony wrist, in a Dickens morality tale,

You turn to me, on our rhetorical armchair, traded
For that chaise longue, when to say French fry

Constituted an infraction, or a senate motion
Up for heated talk on the floor, you take my

Pale hand, hold on for dear life and blurt out
In one breath, as if all the air upped and left:

*We waited too long for this to mean anything.*
*We squandered time as if granted infinite lives.*

*We forgot all about love, the one thing worth*
*Something in a life of little or no value, if*

*The armies on standby mean what they say.*
*None of our actions while apart fed our love.*

Now we are too old to get up from that sofa.
We look at each other and see regret on a skeleton.

Time melts from the fine bones at wrist and ankle,
The seconds ping and ping into a metal bucket,

Planted between us for catching time on the run
To a more worthwhile place with us not there.

*FRED D'AGUIAR*

# Easterly

Lanterns outside The Harbour Inn are visible
come noon from the marshes off Buss Creek.
We crawl behind a trailer-load of beet, shapes fresh
out of cold earth. Creatures at the side of the road curl
like the ones in Narnia turned to stone
by the White Witch – you half-expect them to stretch,
get up and saunter away into the dark stitch
of hawthorn and briar. We're heading east,
hoping to miss the Christmas rush. Another game
of Animal, Vegetable or Mineral is called for.
Heaped bags of Coalite glow unreally on a forecourt
by Darsham Holt. Headlights are set on dipped.
Walkers trudging up along the Blyth's raised bank
are elongated against the red-barred sky
like the soldiers in Lean's *Great Expectations*,
the old black and white one, when they fan out
in the hunt for the convict. It's the weather
for shelter, a bundle of shivers, brandy, that pie.

PETER CARPENTER

# Pip and Magwitch

In an effort to distract his victim and throw the police off his scent,
Anwar al-Awlaki had left a paperback of *Great Expectations*
all bundled up with a printer-cartridge bomb. They found his fingerprints
on the page – wouldn't you know? – where Dickens,
having put us all in a quandary on the great marshes of Kent,
now sets us down with Pip and the leg-ironed convict, Abel Magwitch,
Pip forever chained to Magwitch by dint
of having brought him a pork pie and file in a little care-package.
For the moment, he's a seven-year-old whose Christmas Eve's spent
trying to come up with a way to outfox
this hard-line neighbour, unshaven, the smell of a Polo Mint
not quite masking his breath, his cigar twirling in its unopened sarcophagus
like an Egyptian mummy, one dismissive of the chance
it will ever come into its inheritance.

*PAUL MULDOON*

# Notes on Contributors

*MONIZA ALVI* was born in Pakistan, and grew up in Hertfordshire. She lives in Norfolk. Her six collections of poetry include *The Country at My Shoulder* (1993), shortlisted for the Whitbread Award and the T.S. Eliot poetry prize and *Europa* (2008), also shortlisted for the T.S. Eliot prize. She received a Cholmondeley Award in 2002. *Homesick for the Earth,* versions from Jules Supervielle, appeared in 2011.

*DAVID ANNWN* teaches for the Open University and lives in Wakefield, West Yorkshire. *Bela Fawr's Cabaret* (2008), *Dadadollz* (2010) with Christine Kennedy, and *Ways through Waves* (2011) are amongst his most recent poetry titles. *Gothic Machine* (2011), his study of Gothic literature, early film and lantern-shows of fear, including a discussion of Charles Dickens's phantasmagoria, appeared recently.

*DEREK BEAVEN* was born in 1947. He has always written poetry but is principally a novelist. *Newton's Niece* (1994) won a Commonwealth Writers' Prize and was shortlisted for the Writers' Guild 'Best Fiction Book', *Acts of Mutiny* (1998) was shortlisted for both the Guardian Fiction Prize and the Encore Award and *If the Invader Comes* (2001) was long-listed for the Booker. *His Coldest Winter* was published in 2005. Currently at work on his fifth novel, he is married and lives in Maidenhead.

*ADRIAN BLAMIRES* was born in Cornwall in 1964, and now lives in Reading. His career has mainly involved teaching English in sixth form colleges. His first collection, *The Effect of Coastal Processes* (2005) was a Waterstone's Best New Poetry selection, its title poem read on Radio 4's *Poetry Please*. His latest collection is *The Pang Valley* (2010).

*ROBYN BOLAM* is currently Royal Literary Fund Fellow at Southampton University and Emeritus Professor at St Mary's University College, Twickenham. Her poetry collections are: *The Peepshow Girl* (1989), *Raiding the Borders* (1996), and *New Wings: Poems 1977–2007* (2007), a Poetry Book Society Recommendation. She edited *Eliza's Babes*, an anthology of four centuries of women's poetry in English (2005) and has reviewed for periodicals including the *TLS* and *Poetry Review*.

*ALISON BRACKENBURY*'s most recent collection is *Singing in the Dark* (2008). A selection of new poems can be found on her website: www.alisonbrackenbury.co.uk.

*PETER CARPENTER* has taught English and Creative Writing since 1980, in many places of education including the University of Warwick, the University of Reading, and Tonbridge School; he has also worked for other organisations including Survivors' Poetry, the Arvon Foundation and the Aldeburgh Poetry Festival; since 1997 he has co-directed Worple Press. He has published five collections of poetry and has a New and Selected, *Just Like That*, forthcoming from Smith/Doorstop Books in autumn 2012.

*CONOR CARVILLE* was born in Armagh, N. Ireland. He is a lecturer in English Literature and Creative Writing at the University of Reading. His first volume of poems will be published by Dedalus Press in 2012. A book of criticism, *The Ends of Ireland*, is forthcoming from Manchester University Press also in 2012. He lives in London with his wife and daughter.

*TERRY CREE* is a writer, painter and teacher who lives in Hampshire. He has organised many poetry readings and events down the years and collects modern studio ceramics.

*GERALD DAWE*'s most recent collections are *Lake Geneva* (2003) and *Points West* (2008). His *Selected Poems* will appear in 2012 published by The Gallery Press. He is a Fellow of Trinity College Dublin. Among his other publications, he has edited *Earth Voices Whispering: an anthology of Irish war poetry 1914-1945* (2008) and also published *The Proper Word: Collected Criticism* as well as a memoir, *My Mother City* (both 2007). He lives in County Dublin.

*FRED D'AGUIAR*'s plays include *High Life* (1987) and *A Jamaican Airman Foresees His Death* (1991, and published in 1995). His BBC-commissioned radio play, *Days and Nights in Bedlam*, was broadcast and webcast in October 2005. He is the author of eleven books of poetry and fiction, translated into a dozen languages. Born in London of Guyanese parents and brought up in Guyana, he is the recipient of the Whitbread First Novel Award, the Guyanese Prize for Fiction, and the David Higham Prize. His most recent poetry collection, *Continental Shelf* (2009) was a Poetry Book Society Choice and short-listed for the T. S. Eliot Prize in 2009. He is the Gloria D. Smith Professor at Virginia Tech.

*MAURA DOOLEY*'s most recent collection of poetry is *Life Under Water* (2008). Anthologies of verse and essays she has edited include *The Honey Gatherers: Love Poems* and *How Novelists Work*. She teaches at Goldsmiths College, University of London.

*TIM DOOLEY* is reviews and features editor of *Poetry London* and has worked as a creative writing tutor for Arvon, Writers' Inc and The Poetry School. He has reviewed poetry for the *TLS* and written obituaries for the *Times*. His poems are collected in *Keeping Time* (2008), which was a Poetry Book Society recommendation, and *Imagined Rooms* (2010).

*JANE DRAYCOTT* was nominated as a Next Generation poet. Her collections include *Christina the Astonishing* (with Lesley Saunders) and *Tideway* (with Peter Hay), *Prince Rupert's Drop* (Forward Prize shortlist 1999), *The Night Tree* (PBS Recommendation) and *Over* (T. S. Eliot Prize shortlist 2009). Her translation of the medieval dream-elegy *Pearl*, a Stephen Spender Prize-winner, was published in 2011.

*IAN DUHIG* has written six books of poetry, the latest *Pandorama* (Picador 2010). He also writes short stories, having one in *The New Uncanny* anthology which won a Shirley Jackson Award in 2008, and has worked extensively with musicians, most recently providing texts for Christopher Fox's *Natural Science*, premiered at the Sound Waves Festival in July 2010.

*ANTONY DUNN* has published three collections of poetry, *Pilots and Navigators* (1998), *Flying Fish* (2002) and *Bugs* (2009). He lives in Leeds: www.antonydunn.org.

*CARRIE ETTER* thrice attended The Dickens Project at the University of California, Santa Cruz, and received her PhD in English from the University of California, Irvine. Resident in England since 2001, she is Senior Lecturer in Creative Writing at Bath Spa University and has published two collections of poetry: *The Tethers* (2009), winner of the London Festival Fringe New Poetry Award, and *Divining for Starters* (2011). She also edited *Infinite Difference: Other Poetries by UK Women Poets* (2010).

*ELAINE FEINSTEIN* has lived as a poet, novelist and biographer since 1980. She has received many awards, including a major grant from the Arts Council to write *The Russian Jerusalem*, an innovative mix of prose and poetry (Carcanet, 2008), a Cholmondeley Award, an Honorary D.Litt from the University of Leicester, and a Rockefeller Foundation Fellowship at Bellagio. Her early novel *The Circle* was long-listed for the 'lost' Man Booker Prize in 2010. Her most recent book of poems is *Cities*.

*PETER FINCH* is a full-time poet and psychogeographer. He was born in Cardiff where he still lives. Until recently he was Chief Executive of the writers' society, The Welsh Academy, and later the literature development agency, Literature Wales. He is known for his declamatory poetry readings and his alternative guides to his home city – *Real Cardiff*. His latest collection of poetry is *Zen Cymru*.

*JOHN FULLER*'s *Collected Poems* were published in 1996, and his *Stones and Fires* won the Forward Prize in 1997. The latest two of his six collections of poetry written since then appeared in 2010: *Writing the Picture* (to photographs by David Hurn) from Seren Books, and *Pebble & I* from Chatto and Windus. Chatto also published *Who is Ozymandias? and other puzzles in poetry* in 2011. He was Fellow and Tutor in English at Magdalen College, Oxford, from 1966 to 2002, and is now an Emeritus Fellow.

*ISABEL GALLEYMORE* was born in London in 1988 and holds degrees from the universities of Reading and St Andrews. Her poems have been published in *The Guardian* and *Poetry Review*, and performed at the Royal Festival Hall and Somerset House. She plans to begin a PhD in contemporary poetry and the environment in 2012.

JON GLOVER's last book of poems, *Magnetic Resonance Imaging* (2008), was Ian McMillan's book of the year on BBC's *The Verb*. *Glass Is Elastic* is due from Carcanet in January 2012. He is the Managing Editor of *Stand* and Emeritus Professor of English and Creative Writing at the University of Bolton.

JOHN GREENING's *Hunts: Poems 1979–2009* was published recently by Greenwich Exchange, who have also brought out his *Poets of the First World War* together with his studies of Yeats, Edward Thomas, Hardy, and Ted Hughes. His most recent book is *Poetry Masterclass*. OxfordPoets are to publish his next collection, *To the War Poets*. He received a Cholmondeley Award in 2008 and a Hawthornden Fellowship in 2010. He reviews regularly for the *TLS*. He teaches part-time in Kimbolton, Cambridgeshire.

PHILIP GROSS's latest poetry collections are *The Water Table* – winner of the T.S. Eliot Prize – and *I Spy Pinhole Eye*, with photographer Simon Denison, which won the Wales Book of the Year Award. A new collection, *Deep Field* appeared in 2011. His books of children's poetry include *The All-Nite Café*, which won the Signal Award, while *Off Road To Everywhere* was a PBS Children's Poetry Bookshelf Choice in 2010. Since 2004 he has been Professor of Creative Writing at Glamorgan University. He lives in Penarth.

ALAN HALSEY ran The Poetry Bookshop in Hay-on-Wye from 1979 until 1996. Living in Sheffield since 1997, he continues to work as a poetry bookseller and is the editor of West House Books. His recent collections are *Lives of the Poets* and *Term as in Aftermath*. A new collection, *Even if only out of*, is forthcoming. His edition of Thomas Lovell Beddoes's later poems and fragments, *The Ivory Gate*, appeared in 2011. With Ken Edwards he edited Bill Griffiths's *Collected Earlier Poems* (2010).

A. F. HARROLD has three collections published by Two Rivers Press. For further information visit: www.afharrold.co.uk.

*JOHN HEGLEY* was born in London, educated in Luton, Bristol and at Bradford University. His first professional engagement in the Arts was with Interaction, a North London community arts group where he was engaged as musician and for a children's theatre piece. He now runs work- and play-shops for all ages, alongside performances that retain an interactive style. He has produced books, records, and one mug with his poem about Isambard Kingdom Brunel.

*ALAN JENKINS* is Deputy Editor and Poetry Editor at the *TLS*, and has taught creative writing in the USA, London and Paris. His books of poetry include *Harm* (1994, Forward Prize), *The Drift* (2000), a Poetry Book Society Choice, and *A Shorter Life* (2005), shortlisted for the Forward Prize. *Drunken Boats*, containing his acclaimed translation of Rimbaud's 'Le bateau ivre', was published in 2007. *The Lost World* and *Blue Days (The Sailor's Return)* both appeared last year.

*ANGELA LEIGHTON* is Senior Research Fellow at Trinity College, Cambridge. She has written widely on nineteenth- and twentieth-century poetry, her two most recent critical books being *On Form: Poetry, Aestheticism, and the Legacy of a Word* (2007) and the edited collection, *Voyages over Voices: Critical Essays on Anne Stevenson* (2010). She has published two volumes of poetry: *A Cold Spell* (2000) and *Sea Level* (2007). A third is due in the spring.

*JOHN LUCAS*'s *The Melancholy Man: A Study of Dickens's Novels* was first published in 1970. A second expanded edition appeared ten years later and in 1992, *Dickens: The Major Novels* appeared under the Penguin imprint. He is the author of nine collections of poetry, of many critical studies, and of biographical works. In 2008 his account of contemporary Greece, *92 Acharnon Street*, won the Authors' Club Dolman Best Travel Book Award. Since 1994 he has been publisher/editor of Shoestring Press.

MAIRI MACINNES grew up near Stockton-on-Tees, where she began writing poems. Her poetry and volume of memoirs are available from Shoestring Press.

JAMIE MCKENDRICK has published five books of poetry, most recently *Crocodiles & Obelisks* (2007). He has translated Giorgio Bassani's *The Garden of the Finzi-Continis* (2007), Pier Paolo Pasolini's verse play *Fabrication* (2010), and Valerio Magrelli's poems, *The Embrace* (2009).

PAUL MULDOON's main collections of poetry are *New Weather* (1973), *Mules* (1977), *Why Brownlee Left* (1980), *Quoof* (1983), *Meeting The British* (1987), *Madoc: A Mystery* (1990), *The Annals of Chile* (1994), *Hay* (1998), *Poems 1968–1998* (2001), *Moy Sand and Gravel* (2002), *Horse Latitudes* (2006) and *Maggot* (2010). He writes lyrics for the Princeton-based music collective Wayside Shrines.

KATE NOAKES is a Welsh academician living in Caversham. Her latest collection is *The Wall Menders*. She blogs at www.boomslang poetry.com.

SEAN O'BRIEN's most recent book of poems is *November* (2011), a Poetry Book Society Choice. *The Drowned Book* (2007) won the T. S. Eliot and Forward Prizes. In 2009 his novel *Afterlife* was published. He is Professor of Creative Writing at Newcastle University.

MICHAEL O'NEILL is a Professor of English at Durham University. Recent publications include *Wheel*, a collection of poems (2008) and, as editor, *The Cambridge History of English Poetry* (2010). With Madeleine Callaghan, he has edited *Twentieth-Century British and Irish Poetry: Hardy to Mahon* (2011).

TOM PHILLIPS is a freelance writer living in Bristol. He has published *Burning Omaha* (Firewater, 2002) and *Reversing into the Cold War* (Firewater/Poetry Monthly, 2007). Eight of his plays have been staged in Bristol and Bath, including *Hotel Illyria* (2008), *Arbeit Macht Frei* (2009) and *Man Diving* (2011). His first full collection, *Recreation Ground*, appears this year.

ADRIAN POOLE is Professor of English at the University of Cambridge, and a Fellow of Trinity College, Cambridge. His books include *Shakespeare and the Victorians* (2004) and *Tragedy: A Very Short Introduction* (2005). He has written extensively on nineteenth-century fiction and is editor of the *Cambridge Companion to English Novelists* (2009).

RICHARD PRICE is the author of poetry collections which include *Rays*, *Greenfields*, and *Lucky Day*, the last shortlisted for the Whitbread Poetry Award. He also writes fiction, including the linked short stories *A Boy in Summer* and the novel *The Island*, about a father and daughter who steal a car in an act of revenge. He is Head of Content and Research Strategy at the British Library.

JUSTIN QUINN has published several collections of poetry, most recently *Close Quarters* (2011). He is associate professor of English and American Literature at Charles University, Prague, and has translated the work of several Czech poets, including Petr Borkovec and Ivan Blatný.

DERYN REES-JONES is the author of *Consorting with Angels* and editor of the accompanying anthology *Modern Women Poets*. Her edition of Marie Stopes's novel, *Love's Creation* will be published next year, as will her fourth collection of poems, *Burying the Wren*. In 2010 she received a Cholmondeley Award from the Society of Authors.

PETER RILEY was born in 1940 near Manchester, and has been a teacher and a bookseller. Author of some twenty books and pamphlets of poetry, his *Passing Measures*, a collection of poems, appeared from Carcanet in 2000. His latest books are *Greek Passages* (prose poems) (Shearsman 2009) and *The Glacial Stairway* (Carcanet 2011). His website is at www.aprileye.co.uk.

*PETER ROBINSON* is Professor of English and American Literature at the University of Reading. Among his many books of poetry, criticism and translation are *The Returning Sky* (2012), *Poems* by Antonia Pozzi (2011), and *Poetry & Translation: The Art of the Impossible* (2010). He recently edited Bernard Spencer's *Complete Poetry, Translations & Selected Prose* (2011) and *Reading Poetry: An Anthology* (2011).

*ANTHONY RUDOLF,* born in London in 1942, is the author of books of poetry, literary criticism and autobiography and has also written on the visual arts. He has published translations of books by French and Russian poets. He is Fellow of the Royal Society of Literature and of the English Association. He has been a visiting lecturer and Royal Literary Fund Fellow at universities in the UK, has broadcast on BBC Radio and Television, read his work and lectured in many countries.

*CAROL RUMENS* was born on the Surrey side of the Thames. Her most recent poetry collection is *De Chirico's Threads* (2010). Her awards include the Alice Hunt Bartlett Prize (with Thomas McCarthy). *Holding Pattern* (1998) was short-listed for the Belfast City Arts Award. A Fellow of the Royal Society of Literature, she has published translations, short stories, a novel (*Plato Park*, 1987) and a trio of poetry lectures, *Self into Song* (2007). 'Marshalsea Quadrille' has a form suggested by Paul Muldoon's 'The Rowboat', *Maggot* (2010).

*LESLEY SAUNDERS*, whose prize-winning work has appeared in many magazines and journals, has published two previous books, *Christina the Astonishing* (with Jane Draycott and artist Peter Hay) and *Her Leafy Eye* (with artist Geoff Carr), from Two Rivers Press. Her new collection, *Cloud Camera*, appears from them in 2012.

*ELIZABETH SMITHER* has published fifteen collections of poetry, as well as novels and short stories. She was New Zealand poet laureate (2001–3) and received the Prime Minister's Award for Literary Achievement in Poetry in 2008. Her most recent publications are *The Year of Adverbs* (Auckland University Press, 2007), *Lola* (Penguin, 2010) and *The Commonplace Book: a Writer's Journey through Quotations* (Auckland University Press, 2011).

JULIAN STANNARD has previously lectured at the University of Genoa, and now teaches English and Creative Writing at the University of Winchester. His *The Parrots of Villa Gruber Discover Lapis Lazuli* (Salmon, 2011) comes in the wake of *The Red Zone* (Peterloo, 2007) and *Rina's War* (Peterloo, 2001). He won the Troubadour Prize in 2010.

CHRISTIAN KARLSON STEAD, b. Auckland 1932, has published 13 collections of poems and two of short stories, eleven novels, six books of literary criticism, and edited a number of texts. He was Professor of English at the University of Auckland for twenty years, taking early retirement in 1986. He has won the New Zealand Book Award for both poetry and fiction, the Prime Minister's Award for fiction, the King's Lynn Poetry Prize, the Hippocrates Prize for Poetry and Medicine, and the Sunday Times/E.F.G. Private bank short story award. He was awarded a CBE in 1985 for services to New Zealand literature, elected Fellow of the Royal Society of Literature in 1995, Senior Visiting Fellow at St. John's College, Oxford, in 1996–7, Fellow of the English Association in 2003, and awarded an Honorary Doctorate in Letters by the University of Bristol in 2001. In 2007 he received his country's highest award, the Order of New Zealand.

JAMES SUTHERLAND-SMITH is a poet, translator and reviewer. His most recent collection is *Popeye in Belgrade* (Carcanet, 2008). *Dinner with Fish and Mirrors*, a selection of poems by the Serbian poet Ivana Milankova, translated with Zorica Petrovic, is due from Arc Publications. He reviews for *PN Review* and *The Bow-Wow Shop*.

GEORGE SZIRTES has written some fourteen books of poetry and has translated roughly the same number of books of poetry or fiction from the Hungarian. He was awarded the Geoffrey Faber award for his first book, *The Slant Door* (1979) and the T.S. Eliot Prize for *Reel* (2004), for which he was also shortlisted in 2009, for *The Burning of the Books*. His *New and Collected Poems* was published in 2008.He was trained as an artist and now teaches at the University of East Anglia.

SUSAN UTTING has taught poetry and creative writing for many years, chiefly at Reading and Oxford Universities, and for Randolph Macon Women's College. Poetry books include *Something Small is Missing* (1999) and *Striptease* (2001) from Smith/ Doorstop and two collections from Two Rivers Press: *Houses Without Walls* (2006) and *Fair's Fair* (2012). www.susanutting.co.uk.

JEFFREY WAINWRIGHT's poetry is published by Carcanet Press, most recently *Clarity or Death!* (2008). His critical work includes a book on the poetry of Geoffrey Hill, *Acceptable Words* (2005) and *Poetry: the Basics* (second edition 2011). A new collection of poems, *The Reasoner*, is due in 2012. He lives in Manchester.

GREGORY WOODS is professor of gay and lesbian studies at Nottingham Trent University. His critical monographs, including *A History of Gay Literature* (1998), are published by Yale University Press. His poetry collections, the latest of which is *An Ordinary Dog* (2011), are published by Carcanet Press.

KIT WRIGHT lives in East London. *Hoping It Might Be So* is his most recent volume of poems for adults. *The Magic Box* collects his verse for children.

Two Rivers Press has been publishing in and about Reading since 1994. Founded by the artist Peter Hay (1951–2003), the press continues to delight readers, local and further afield, with its varied list of individually designed, thought-provoking books.